THE BRAIN HUT

THE BRAIN HUT

THE IMPORTANCE
OF PROACTIVITY AND
INTENTIONALITY

NICHOLAS D'SOUZA

NEW DEGREE PRESS

THE BRAIN HUT

The Importance of Proactivity and Intentionality

ISBN   978-1-63676-612-6   *Paperback*

           978-1-63676-280-7   *Kindle Ebook*

           978-1-63676-281-4   *Ebook*

To God.

CONTENTS

———

"The brain is the most valuable weapon in the midst of all adversity and fear."

—NICHOLAS D'SOUZA

INTRODUCTION

———

*"In my mind, I was always afraid, but I had this voice that
would always be battling me, saying, 'Hey, you have to get up
and do something.'"*[1]

—DAVID GOGGINS

David Goggins did not have an easy start in life. He grew
up with an abusive father and was bullied in school, where
he also struggled with a learning disability. Goggins had
always ignored the voice in his head that offered encouragement. Struggle was a fear, and comfort was the easy route. By
his early twenties, Goggins had packed two hundred nine-
ty-seven pounds onto his six foot one frame and was working
for a pest control company; a job that he hated.

"I had two options," he said. "I would either be that three
hundred-pound guy who sprayed for cockroaches and made

———

1   *PowerfulJRE*, "Joe Rogan Experience #1080 - David Goggins," February
19, 2018, video, 1:54:22.

a thousand dollars a month at twenty-four years old, or I could totally just suck it up and fail and fail until I succeed."[2]

When he was younger, Goggins would watch the movie *Rocky* over and over again. In the final fight scene, Rocky gets beaten up badly, but he would not stay down. "He was a dumb fighter," Goggins said. "He couldn't read, he couldn't write, and that was me. It was the face of Apollo Creed that changed my life. I wanted to be the guy that was going to keep going after whatever was in front of him. I wanted to feel something besides defeat."[3]

Goggins found his purpose by dropping the excess weight and becoming a Navy SEAL. He went further to become an endurance athlete, racking up many accomplishments such as setting a Guinness World Record for doing the most pull-ups in twenty-four hours or running two hundred five miles in twenty-four hours. Overall, he competed in over sixty endurance events and placed in the top five of all of them. Goggins is now known as "the World's Toughest Man."

Goggins' story shows that one's accomplishments can be reached by creating intentions and producing a proactive approach for execution. He could have reflected on the past hard times of his life and been discouraged, thinking he was a nobody for the rest of his life. However, he had hope and took a proactive mentality to perpetually conquer the goals he set before himself. But it all started with him. His intentions were internal, and that is a major concept of this book.

---

2   *Ibid.*

3   *JRE Clips,* "Joe Rogan - David Goggins Journey From 300 lbs to a Navy Seal," February 19, 2018, video, 22:25

* * *

I grew up thinking that the more education someone had, the more successful they would be. David Goggins considered himself illiterate and cheated his way through high school. Unlike Goggins, I attribute my current success to the mental skills I learned in school. However, I realize that no matter how educated I am, my credentials and knowledge will not magically make me successful. Each of us must harness a combination of education and life experience and use them to set intentions and be proactive by going after what we want in life.

When I was a competitive swimmer in college, I loved to watch motivational videos, which led to reading self-help books. A year ago, I realized that I didn't feel like I had a calling or purpose in life. I was unemployed and lost. My biggest fear was that I'd someday regret the choices I've made and the choices I did not make. So, to create a better person, I wanted to go through the pain and suffering now to create a much better self in the future. Pain and suffering can pertain to different meanings. Whether it means sacrificing something for the sake of a better activity or working out ruthlessly, there is a respective degree of tribulation to pass through to get to the next level.

During my time of hardships, I decided to permanently delete all my social media accounts. This was a "pain" since I had a daily habit of posting and scrolling through my social media feed. However, I had to do what was necessary to focus on my reality and stay away from the superficial. Hence, pain can be mental along with physical. There was also bad pain in being unemployed. This gave me a good kick to get on the move and search more deeply into the job market. Both the good and bad suffering in life can motivate us to achieve higher goals. Of course, there must be some relaxation and good feelings along the successful journey. However, perpetual comfort will lead to unhealthy complacency.

I feel compelled to write this book because I have always thrived on motivation and harnessing struggle to obtain specific objectives. I have read several self-help books this past year and I want to introduce my own concept of "the Brain Hut" with some content from these books. I believe the Brain Hut model will give new insight on how you can give perspective to different facets of your life.

* * *

"When you think you're done, you're only at forty percent of your body's capability." —David Goggins

While I was thinking about David Goggins' forty percent rule, I thought of the primitive nature of the brain which likes comfort. I realized the more I face adversity, the more I can extend past that forty percent level and learn how sophisticated my brain's function can be. Even though the nature of the subconscious mind can be complex, the simple, intentional ideas of our conscious mind can be conducive to great actions.

During this thinking process, the term "hut" popped into my mind. A hut is simple and resonates with the primitive nature of the brain. I thought of the ways I could overcome procrastination. Why not make a simple model named the "Brain Hut?" I thought of adding some "rooms" in this Hut diagram to give a unique representation of how we can harness our brain as a weapon to execute our goals in an efficient and timely manner.

As I continued to write about procrastination, technology, human relationships, and critical thinking, I decided to base all my writing around my model.

You will enjoy this book if you are a motivated individual searching for a calling or a direction in your life, as well as if you have a relevant background of the neuroscience of our brains.

In this book, I will discuss harnessing our education with intention, share insights from some of the world's most successful people, share personal experiences and stories from primary interviews, and ultimately, provide my own map on the principles I have developed.

I believe we can get distracted by all the noise around us. However, by harnessing the principles of proactivity and intentionality, we can produce much greater versions of ourselves!

PART 1

HOW WE
GOT HERE

CHAPTER 1

THE FLAW IN THE EDUCATION SYSTEM

———

"Don't confuse schooling with education. I didn't go to Harvard but the people that work for me did."

—ELON MUSK

I believe that education has made me who I am today. I learned what I needed to do to complete my assignments on time and get good grades. Mathematics was my greatest strength, and I enjoyed excelling in each course I took. I took pride in improving in the subjects I considered to be my weaknesses. I believe I earned a valuable college degree from Fordham University and view it as a reflection of my hard work and efforts.

A few years after college graduation, however, I realized there was something empty inside of me. I was working full-time, but for the first time, I didn't have grades to guide my work. I had this feeling that I was meant to do something more. I knew that I needed to be more proactive because opportunities and success will not magically come to me. I needed to act in advance to create opportunities to succeed. I also needed to be deliberate and act with intention because I can create my future. Nobody else will do the work for me.

I believe that the school system has a major flaw. It failed to teach me how to program my mind for success through the principles of proactivity and intentionality. Yes, I did learn and grow through the structured courses in the education system, but I didn't have the freedom to create my own goals and to learn to take risks to meet them. My goal in school was to achieve high grades, but because I would be disappointed if I failed a test or a class, I avoided as many mistakes as possible. I became a perfectionist.

Eventually, I discovered some of the greatest success stories from podcasts and books. These lessons taught me that the school system misses the greatest assets every single person should chase—risks and failure. In school, I tried to minimize mistakes for the sake of academic rewards. However, I realized that through failure and risks, I can learn more and feel comfortable failing, which leads to growth. In order for me to do this, I must set my own goals and be willing to fail to build upon great successes and knowledge. I believed that my college degree would magically make me successful, and my good grades would give me the innate ability to succeed in any endeavor I chose. The reality, though, is that education is a lifetime work that is not limited to the school system.

David Goggins is now known as one of the most iconic Navy SEALs of all time, but he considered himself to be illiterate and cheated his way throughout high school. He created the forty percent rule—that most people are only living up to forty percent of their true capability. Goggins based his concept on his own experiences of pain and suffering.

Mel Robbins got her undergraduate degree from an Ivy League school but was unemployed and stressed out at age forty-one. She developed the five-second rule to help her beat her procrastination habits—her theory being if someone counts down from five to one, the brain will trigger the person to immediately wake up.

Napoleon Hill is an iconic self-help author who exemplifies the belief in high-quality principles being an avenue for success. Through Napoleon Hill's work, I learned how Henry Ford, who had nothing more than an elementary education, was able to set goals and meet them in the most efficient way possible.

Goggins, Robbins, and Ford are only three of the many great people I have learned from. All their stories have the same idea—to be proactive and intentional in creating success. Neither a limited education nor prestigious education will predict success or failure. Success comes from the mind. I have the ability to create my own education for a lifetime.

***

Education is a never-ending journey of embracing failure and self-accountability to meet goals. However, at its core, education has one of two ways of affecting you:

- Your academic achievements define your talent in the real world.
- Your academic achievements are just statistics. Regardless of how well or poorly you did in school, your potential for growth is limitless.

American psychologist Carol S. Dweck portrays two separate mindsets in the perspective of success and believes that students have one of these different mindsets: the fixed mindset and the growth mindset.

The fixed mindset is how we harness our school achievements as a credible indicator of our future success.

Dweck says, "Believing that your qualities are carved in stone—the fixed mindset—creates an urgency to prove yourself over and over. If you have only a certain amount of intelligence, a certain personality, and a certain moral character—well, then you'd better prove that you have a healthy dose of them. It simply wouldn't do to look or feel deficient in these most basic characteristics."[4]

Just as the term "fixed" indicates, this approach is limited. These people are desperate to fill the empty gaps for the sake of self-validation. They want to maintain whatever grand identity they choose whether it is realistic or not.

Opposite to the fixed mindset is Dweck's theory of the growth mindset.

---

4   Carol S. Dweck, *Mindset: The New Psychology of Success* (New York: Penguin Random House, 2006, 2016), 5–6, Google Books.

"In this mindset," Dweck says, "the hand you're dealt is just the starting point for development. Basic qualities can be cultivated through efforts, strategies, and help from others." According to Dweck, "Although people may differ in every which way in their initial talents and aptitudes, interests, or temperaments everyone can change and grow through application and experience."[5]

While I did learn some principles of intention and proactivity in school, I was not setting my own goals and applying the principles to meet them. I had a fixed mindset where I had to validate my academic status by meeting the school's goals for me. Failure was something to be avoided. Through the growth mindset, however, I am free to set whatever goals I want and be willing to fail and fail until I succeed. Along the way, I am earning a valuable education. I labeled myself a failure through my failures in school. However, I now label myself a learner through my failures in the real world because they are lessons to me.

Dweck talks about how the fixed and growth mindsets are relevant in the corporate culture. She says, "Employees in the fixed-mindset companies not only say that their companies are less likely to support them in risk-taking and innovation, they are also far more likely to agree that their organizations are rife with cutthroat or unethical behavior."[6] On the other hand, Dweck says that supervisors in growth-mindset companies rated their employees as more collaborative and more committed to learning and growing, adding that "these are

---

5   Ibid. 6–8.
6   Ibid. 142.

all things that make a company more agile and more likely to stay in the vanguard."[7]

I find the growth mindset much more compelling than the fixed mindset. I can fail ten times at something, but perhaps that's the number of lessons I need to succeed for the first time. If I had a fixed mindset, then I would feel discouraged by my first failure and avoid persevering through a rigorous process. Ideally, the fixed mindset should be avoided as it does not have much positive influence on the mind. It is limited and does not have an aspect of exploration and hope as the growth mindset does.

An entrepreneurial mindset is both intentional and proactive. My academic status, my credentials, and other people are not going to do the work for me! I define the fixed mindset as if I am urgently trying to cover up and resolve a flaw just to let go of any negative reputation. The growth mindset is about taking a step back in every failure and harnessing the mind and patience to use the failure as a stepping stone for potential growth. The growth mindset is about finding joy in the struggle.

Author Eric Barker believes school success does not guarantee someone will be successful in life. Class valedictorians do not always succeed. In a study done at Boston College, researcher Karen Arnold followed eighty-one high school valedictorians and salutatorians after graduation. Of the ninety-five percent who went on to college, only sixty percent graduated. Barker says that there was little debate that high school success predicted college success. However, Barker

7   Ibid. 142.

asks, "How many of these number one high school performers go on to change the world, run the world, or impress the world? The answer seems to be clear: zero."[8]

Barker explains why he thinks that education doesn't promote real-world applications for learning: "School has clear rules. Life often doesn't. When there's no clear path to follow, academic high achievers break down."[9] Barker cites Shawn Anchor's research at Harvard, which he says "shows that college grades aren't any more predictive of subsequent life success than rolling dice. A study of over seven hundred American millionaires showed their average college GPA was 2.9."[10]

* * *

When I read about the successful people who acted with intention, I realized that I needed to stop leaning on my past academic achievements. I finished college with a 3.2 GPA. Does that mean I am set to become a successful millionaire? No. However, if I harness the lessons I learned in school and throughout my life experiences, I have limitless potential. I must be willing to learn through risks and failures, though. I create my own goals and set out to achieve them through a hard mindset. I create my own destiny.

So, what are two principles which are relevant to a successful life in the post-academic world? Proactivity and intentionality!

---

8   Eric Barker, *Barking Up the Wrong Tree: The Surprising Science Behind Why Everything You Know About Success Is (Mostly) Wrong* (Harper One, 2017), 10–12, Google Books.

9   Ibid. 10–12.

10 Ibid. 10–12.

CHAPTER 2

WHY ARE PROACTIVITY AND INTENTIONALITY IMPORTANT?

———

"Proactive people carry their own weather with them."

—STEPHEN R. COVEY

In Chapter One, I mentioned how my education will not magically guide me down the road to success. I stress the importance of proactivity and intentionality because it awakens my untapped potential. The terms "proactive" and "intention" may sound vague. I can be proactive and intentional to act on a bad idea or a good idea. This book focuses on gravitating our intentions toward good ideas.

I do not see success as an end in and of itself. I view consistent effort throughout life, despite victories and failures, as the true definition of success. This requires an exercise of the principles of intentionality and proactivity. I can delude myself into thinking that greatness will serve me naturally the older I get. However, decades from now, I will not have as many future years to be optimistic about. Instead, I will look back more in retrospect, regretting the tasks I did not do. The worst pain I can imagine in my lifetime is the pain of regret. And when reality hits during this pain, I would acknowledge that I would be the person to blame for not acting on what I felt I had to offer.

One of life's greatest questions is "Why am I who I am?" I will never know the answer to my given identity. However, I do have the power to create a "new me" through my internal efforts. In consistent practice, I am transforming myself and seeing a new me every time I view my image in the mirror because I sense a different person after going through a valuable struggle. I am deluded to think that someone else will give me the magic source for change. Only one person can do this for me—the person reflected in the mirror. I always see room for improvement.

As the philosopher Socrates once said, "The only true wisdom is in knowing you know nothing." Everyone is dealt different cards in life. Some have it better than others. Personally, just the thought that someone else does not have granted access to life's necessities makes me feel empowered to act upon my blessings and opportunities. In a way, I am doing that unfortunate person a favor, and it brings me happiness. Let's go into the definitions and the reasons that proactivity and intentionality are important.

INTENTIONALITY

By intentionality, I refer to the idea that I am responsible for deliberately making my choices; all my decisions come from within. I will never know what hardships or unprecedented circumstances I will fall into. Therefore, with an intentional mindset, I am more competent for what life throws at me. Canadian psychologist Jordan Peterson has an interesting concept of standing up straight with one's shoulders back. It is a way to inspire someone to be audacious and bold.

He notes the rewards of this practice by saying that "people, including yourself, will start to assume that you are competent and able."[11] Based on this positive feedback, Peterson says, "You will be less anxious."[12] After accomplishing an admiring feat, I find no greater feeling than to say, "I created this. Nobody held my hand to do this or that. I harnessed my intentions and just went after it!" In order to emit good deeds, we need to have full confidence in ourselves because our internal strength is where our intentions lie.

This good feeling begs for more intention and less favor of complacency. Peterson says, "Your conversations will flow better...this will make you more likely to meet people, interact with them, and impress them. Doing so will not only genuinely increase the probability that good things will happen to you, but it will also make those good things feel better when they do happen."[13]

---

11   Jordan Peterson, 12 *Rules for Life: An Antidote to Chaos*, (Toronto: Penguin Random House Canada Limited, 2018), 59, Google Books.

12   Ibid.

13   Ibid.

I acknowledge the social perspective as a motivator for taking intentions on my purpose. When I hear about someone else's major feats, I gain some respect for their discipline and will to chase after their goals no matter what obstacles get in their way. I warn myself not to emulate their demeanor as much as observe the principles they put into practice. It is fine to meditate on a successful person's enthusiasm for that "kick" to gain momentum toward reaching a certain goal, but everyone has their own personal "Why" for accomplishing something. The only person who can help me figure that out is me because I need to connect the dots of my past to understand what can bolster me into action. This works because nobody else has walked in my shoes before but me. I live my world in my brain and my brain stores my personal conversations for only myself. Therefore, nobody else can truly understand my life's calling from a holistic standpoint. Philosopher John Locke says, "...we should make greater progress in the discovery of rational and contemplative knowledge, if we sought it in the fountain, in the consideration of things themselves, and made use rather of our own thoughts, than other men's to find it."[14] Successful people's inspiring emotions are not enough to motivate one's self to keep moving forward. The "Why" should be a personal matter placed deep in one's heart.

As long as I am alive on this planet, I have the time to exercise and develop a robust brain through intentionally educating myself. I find joy in inspiring others to find self-knowledge

---

14   John Locke, *An Essay Concerning Human Understanding* (Indianapolis: Hackett Publishing Company, 1996), 67–69, Google Books.

for themselves through my actions, as opposed to simply providing trite talk without action.

I will have downs, through my intentions, but the downs do not have me. I need to be deliberate in order to persevere during my failures and focus on fulfilling my intentions.

PROACTIVITY

By proactivity, I refer to taking the initiative in creating and carrying out a goal which will make me realize my strengths. If I intend to be proactive after a goal, I look at the goal as just a small puzzle piece in answering my big, aspiration questions: "How much quality and how many lives can I inspire during my time on this planet?" People always want to know how successful people get where they are. All success is based on an intention and a proactive approach to get it based on internal will. Through this, successful people can motivate others to find their passion even if it means being patient for quite some time.

Sometimes I meditate on death and imagine a video of my life as one big risk (from an afterlife perspective). There is so much sophistication in my mental and physical features, yet my life is vulnerable to end at any time of any day. It is as if I feel that I am destined to find much more of my identity, but Time is not guaranteed. This idea propels me to exercise the proactive mindset and not fall into a meaningless trap of complacency. Every day and every opportunity are risks to improve and show greatness. Psychologist Tasha Eurich says, "While goals can leave us feeling deflated and disappointed once we've achieved them, aspirations are never fully completed; we can get up every morning feeling motivated by them all over again."[15] Proactivity is not a one-time asset which magically sets us up for more adversities along the road. It is a lifestyle.

I view my life as a gift. Gifts are typically not expected, unless on major holidays. Gratitude is the most important value to have in order to obtain anything sanguine in our lives. Therefore, I have to capitalize on my created intentions and take responsibility to create the perpetual discipline of exercising valuable principles. Only I can decide what to direct my purpose toward. However, I must be cognizant of how every risk may involve a trial and error approach. Through this proactive action, I can gain more knowledge about my strengths and weaknesses. Personally, I focus on doubling down on my strengths. There are others who may find greatness in focusing on how to overcome their weaknesses.

Proactivity is a daily exercise because some of the greatest processes take months or years to complete. If I give one hundred percent effort one day toward a goal, then I may have just moved one percent forward toward the finish line. As important as this continual process is, I must consciously maintain the purpose of chasing every feat. Every day is not the same. There may be so much noise in my environment that I subconsciously lose my initial intention in the process. Proactivity does not necessarily mean moving forward one hundred fifteen miles per hour one hundred percent of the time.

---

15   Tasha Eurich, *Insight: The Surprising Truth About How Others See Us, How We See Ourselves, and Why the Answers Matter More Than We Think* (New York: Penguin Random House, 2017), 23–24, Google Books.

I can be doing everything right, but there may come a time when I need to take that step back for rejuvenation. Philosopher Norman Drummond says, "A life spiraling out of control, at the mercy of external pressures, has no space for joy or wisdom. It is perfectly normal for busy people to feel overwhelmed by the demands of life now and then, but to feel that way is a warning sign and to ignore it is to rush headlong toward unhappiness and ill health."[16]

Sometimes I find myself responding to others' social bonding requests by saying, "I can't. I have lots of work to do." This may be a valid excuse in urgent times, but not necessarily all the time. After all, I may have still had the appropriate time to give my one hundred percent on a task and get it done had I decided to join my friends for some time. The typical mantra I respond to them with may merely produce a proactive sense in me. However, saying something and doing it are not always symbiotic. I have to be cognizant that the more proactive and efficient I am during a certain task, the more comfortable my brain gets the next time I approach it.

Therefore, my mantra excuse may just reflect an unsuccessful attempt on a certain previous task. There should always be some sanguine approach after a success, and even after a failure. Psychology professor Art Markman says, "Whenever you do something successful, mechanisms in your brain relate the action you performed to the situation in which you performed it. That way, when the situation comes up again,

---

16 Norman Drummond, *Step Back: Why You Need to Stop What You're Doing to Really Start Living* (UK: Hodder & Stoughton, 2015), 15–17, Google Books.

your brain can suggest that you perform the same action."[17] This promotes the idea that our active intentions can store so much knowledge in our brains, and it is so important for a shift in perspective and confidence to experience even more. If you helped an injured person cross the road, then you feel a great feeling of impact. This feeling will linger on for a long time since it is a source of inspiration. Similarly, the proactive approach to embark on a constructive process will insert diverse information in the brain. When we revisit a task for improvement, we are not starting from scratch but from experience.

Since life is so short, I want to chase after every possible endeavor I am called for. It is important that I don't reflect so much on past credentials or achievements superfluously, but to instead be proactive on new goals time after time and work as if I have accomplished nothing before. This is what creates the hunger to be proactive.

REGRET IS THE WORST PAIN

I previously mentioned the pain of regret. Without a proactive and intentional lifestyle, I view regret as the worst pain imaginable. There is brutal pain, in every aspect, toward big and tough goals. However, the pain of regret is distinct because it comes right after you realize you didn't capitalize on an opportunity within a certain time frame. The worst degree of this is much later in life when one does not have the physical capabilities to make up for this regret.

---

17   Art Markman, *Smart Change: Five Tools to Create New and Sustainable Habits in Yourself and Others,* (New York: Penguin Group, 2014), 5–6, Google Books.

I contemplate on all the opportunities I did not create, saying, "I could have done this. What if I did this?" "What if" is the worst thing to say after it is too late. I view "procrastination" as the best term to describe this pitiful lifestyle, lacking in eagerness and fulfillment.

Procrastination, just like proactivity, is done voluntarily. However, the two respectively pertain to different ends. Proactivity is now and procrastination is later. Dr. Piers Steel defines the background of the term "procrastination" by saying, "Procrastination comes from the Latin *pro,* which means 'forward, forth, or in favor of,' and *crastinus,* which means 'of tomorrow.'"[18]

Proactivity does not necessarily mean I have to act today. If I have the courage to act on a thought, then just noting my plans for another day and committing to them is a proactive move. It deals with wisdom and patience. These terms that sound slow and delayed do not align with procrastination. Procrastination is a refusal to make the right mental or physical step toward a goal. Patience and wisdom wait for the most efficient time to execute or take a step back. This relates to what I mentioned earlier about a consistent and efficient process on the road of proactivity. When I procrastinate, I comfort myself with the feeling that it will be done and the good feeling I will have after I complete it. However, I am not necessarily thinking about the "how" behind the process. When I am patient, I am focused on my game plan to execute something which is yet to come to fruition. As Abraham

---

18   Piers Steel, *The Procrastination Equation: How to Stop Putting Things Off and Start Getting Stuff Done,* (HarperCollins e-books, 2010), 16-18, Google Books.

Lincoln once said: "Give me six hours to chop down a tree and I will spend the first four sharpening the ax." I imagine my goals as a tree which I want to execute in a high-quality fashion. Therefore, proactivity involves preparation in addition to execution.

GOD VS. DOG

I have this concept of "god vs. dog." The term "god" is not defined in the divine sense like "God." Instead, it relates to mastering something, or being intentional about it. If you reverse the "d" and "g" in god, you get dog. Just as a dog obeys its owner, I view this analogy as pertaining to a reactive circumstance for the sake of survival. For example, if a person is proactive in climbing the corporate ladder, then he will be willing to work more than he is paid to do. On the other hand, if a person does the minimum amount of work, then he may be reactive to an unprecedented poor evaluation, indicating that he is of no interest for a promotion.

Every decision we make in our present contributes to our future. Nothing external will give you what you need just because you might think it should. There are principles to exercise on this journey, as well as principles which serve as caveats to get us sidetracked. In Part Two, I will reveal these principles and elaborate on them with a self-made map in the beginning of Part Three!

PART 2

THE NEUROSCIENCE AND IMPORTANCE OF SIX PRINCIPLES

CHAPTER 1

GOOD HABITS

———

"Good habits are the key to all success. Bad habits are the unlocked door to failure."

–OG MANDINO

Throughout my academic career, I was in the habit of studying for exams and training almost every day for competitive swimming. After I graduated college, I had a weird transition into the real world and felt lost. I had a job, but a part of me still felt like I was growing as a student athlete. I had to go through trial and error stages on different tasks, outside of work, to find a new passion. In other words, I needed to find a new hobby.

In retrospect, I view my first couple of years out of college as a total waste for opportunity. I was not building any type of good habit, which would help me grasp a potential opportunity. Experiences bring about new habits and development in certain areas we want to improve. Therefore, if I wanted to get on a strict regimen, I had to be proactive in stepping out there and fixating on that passion! As actor Bruce Lee once said, "I fear not the man who has practiced ten thousand kicks once, but I fear the man who has practiced one kick ten thousand times."

The greater I grow in something, the more I want to grow. There are no limits to habits. Author Stephen Covey notes the powerful mental transition that good habits can give us over bad habits. He says, "Breaking deeply embedded, habitual tendencies such as procrastination…or selfishness that violate basic principles of human effectiveness involves more than a little willpower and a few minor changes in our lives. "'Lift off' takes a tremendous effort, but once we break out of the gravity pull, our freedom takes on a whole new dimension."[19] Covey's statement speaks volumes on the power of intentionality and our internal courage to change our reflection in the mirror into a new self-made individual. Thinking that change will happen is different than habitually practicing to make that change occur.

There is a process to make that proactive change.

- First, it starts with a belief that a certain goal can be possible. Beliefs are so important because they add fuel to our passions and mold our personal feelings throughout the day.
- It is prudent to find the right words to establish a game plan. A certain mantra or set of powerful words can be harnessed through a habit to remind oneself of the initial purpose.

---

19   Stephen R. Covey, *The 7 Habits of Highly Effective People* (Miami: FranklinCovey, 2015), 51–53, Google Books.

- Action is then necessary to bring the talk to fruition.
- The next key step is habit. It feels good to embark on a journey, but consistency is important; consistency is habit.
- Naturally, a positive change will occur whether your goals result in success or failure. I like this quote from author Jim N. Watkins: "A river cuts a rock, not because of its power, but because of its persistence." A good effort one day is only a big step toward the end goal. Habits are a long-term game. Beliefs turn to words. Words turn to action. Action turns to habit. And habits turn to change.

Proactivity leads to happiness when someone sees the habitual work pay off. Happiness is a free feeling and opens endless possibilities to connect to other habits. However, I need to be cognizant of how one habit may affect another habit. For example, if I want to get into the habit of exercising well, then I have to get into the habit of eating healthy to improve my physical stamina and strength. If I choose to eat junk food and do intense workouts, I do not have the integrity to fulfill my end goal.

Habits are not developed for the sake of going through the motions. Courage will get the habit started, but it is inevitable that the integrity will die if other adjustments are not made. Dr. Tamsin Astor says, "Willpower can be trained, but it does get fatigued. My approach to creating connections between habits essentially works by reducing the willpower element because you start to connect your new habits with current habits that are serving you."[20] I view Dr. Astor's statement as

---

20 Tamsin Astor, Force of Habit: Unleash Your Power by Developing Great Habits (Florida: Mango Publishing Company, 2018), 40–42, Google Books.

another way of saying, "Train smart, not hard." Habits get me in the loop of intentionality. However, I may easily lose sight of my purpose one day and fall back if I do not have another symbiotic habit to set my whole day straight.

Good habits indicate a proactive lifestyle and well-judged decision-making. It is easy to fall for expedient, bad decisions which make me feel "good." The brain reads any form of a habit as a habit, regardless if it's good or bad. Dr. Richard O'Connor says, "Each time we engage in a bad habit, we make it more likely we'll do it again in the future. But in the same way, each time we engage in a good habit, we make it more likely that we'll do it again."[21]

I struggle in gravitating toward good habits due to their slow and disciplined nature. I feel much more satisfaction in reacting to a pleasing task instead. O'Connor says, "Focused attention and practice…will change the brain's reward system, so that bad habits will lose their appeal and be replaced by new, self-constructive behavior patterns…. Every day you practiced left its traces in the brain; you can get back on the horse after a fall and expect it soon to be as easy and rewarding as ever."[22] Proactivity is like taking the right number of risks to get the brain into a habitual trance to overcome the setbacks along the journey.

The basal ganglia are the part of the brain responsible for storing habits. Author Charles Duhigg notes a study from

---

21 Richard O'Connor, *Rewire: Change Your Brain to Break Bad Habits, Overcome Addictions, Conquer Self-Destructive Behavior* (New York: Penguin Group, 2014), 6-7, Google Books.

22 Ibid.

the early 1990s known among MIT researchers as studying the basal ganglia in rats, which were placed in a T-shaped maze with chocolate at one end. Once the maze's partition opened, the rat was in an aimless and illogical stroll. "...it would usually wander up and down the center aisle, sniffing in corners and scratching at walls. It appeared to smell chocolate but couldn't figure out how to find it."[23] The basal ganglia activity proved an interesting study, as it suggested "each time a rat sniffed the air or scratched a wall, its brain exploded with activity, as if analyzing each new scent, sight, and sound. The rat was processing information the entire time it meandered."[24]

The first step in any process may feel empty and even be the hardest to take. This is what makes proactivity such a powerful weapon because it indicates the great courage it takes to initiate a new process of habit. As the habit evolves, the courage tends to diminish into an effortless state. Eventually, after a couple days of repetition in the maze, the rat's mental activity decreased and it "didn't need to scratch the walls or smell the air anymore."[25] Within a week, the rat "had internalized how to sprint through the maze to such a degree that it hardly needed to think at all" to reach the chocolate.[26]

Sometimes when I look back at my major improvements in both school and swimming, I think of what "magic" it took

---

23 Charles Duhigg, *The Power of Habit: Why We Do What We Do in Life and Business* (New York: Penguin House, 2012), 23–25, Google Books.
24 Ibid.
25 Ibid.
26 Ibid.

for me to develop new skills. But with contemplative thought, I realized the journeys to my improvements felt similar to my journeys toward mediocrity: they either had good or bad habits and felt normal. Good habits are established by a consistent proactive mindset to knock down the early unknown fundamentals and develop a new mindset.

On the other hand, a disruption in this habit can ruin the momentum. Have you ever forgotten your school locker code or work laptop password after a long vacation? This is because the weekly habit was replaced by a new, temporary daily habit of complacency in the vacation. Every Sunday night, I can rehearse my habits for the upcoming week. The thrill in the escape from normalcy throws this habit away and it requires self-accountability to readjust and return to one's old habits.

I find that the beauty in habit is that it evolves the proactive mindset from a thinking aspect to more of a commitment aspect. Once I register hard work and proper technique into a habit, then intentionality should be my only concern in growing with a certain endeavor. I think less and simply show up more. This is what makes habit the exercise for proactivity—it provides the right direction from the very beginning of the process. Habitual direction involves prior experiences.

Philosopher William Ockham said, "When two phenomena appear together or in succession with such consistency that whenever one of them is posited the other invariably appears also, and whenever the former is not posited the latter does not appear, then it can be concluded that a causal link exists between the two. Habits function thus with regard to certain acts."[27]

If I am not proactive on a personal goal of mine, then I can only think and think about it, only to lead to overthinking. It is easy to think of developing habits and working toward the end goal. However, being proactive is different than being inactive. When I put overthinking into perspective, I imagine dark clouds hovering underneath the sun on what would otherwise be a gorgeous and cloudless day. This is because I feel saddened that I cannot react to a magical and external force to get me started on a rigorous process.

Even though proactive habits relate to action, habits can be mental as well, especially for overthinking or inaction. Psychiatrist Jeffrey M. Schwartz refers to inaction as "anything that you do repeatedly that is caused by a deceptive brain message and takes you away from focusing on something that is beneficial to you."[28] The proactive first step is the antidote for inactivity! I have to be vulnerable to fail and learn to obtain a habit. Doing something is better than doing nothing.

Through habits, not only does the cognitive aspect diminish, but the emotional flavor does too. Dr. Jeremy Dean says, "Like anything in life, as we become habituated, our emotional response lessens. The emotion researcher Nico Frijda

---

27 Oswald Fuchs, *The Psychology of Habit According to William Ockham* (Oregon: Wipf and Stock Publishers, 2016), 7, Google Books.

28 Jeffrey M. Schwartz and Rebecca Gladding, *You Are Not Your Brain: The 4-Step Solution for Changing Bad Habits, Ending Unhealthy Thinking, and Taking Control of Your Life* (New York: Penguin Group, 2011), 16–18, Google Books.

classifies this as one of the laws of emotion and it applies to both pleasure and pain."[29]

I start any new proactive endeavor in a gamut of different emotions saying, "Where am I going with this?" However, practicality completely kicks out this question from context the further I grow in the endeavor. Everything is normal and may possibly end up being mundane unless I have a purpose driven intention. Habits are the base of our intentions. If I have a habit of arriving to work on time, then it indicates I am intentional on starting the day organized.

Dr. Jeremy Dean says, "We all have an intuitive sense that our habits are built up purely in the service of our goals…remember that bad habits are also goal-oriented, although the goal may not be a good one, like getting drunk to forget one's problems…the stronger people's habits, the more they believe that those habits are goal-oriented."[30] My habits interconnect with my other habits. If I have a strong bad habit, then it can poorly affect the nascent stage of a good habit. Also, I have to be cognizant of the types of thrills I experience with my habits. I can feel "good" after acting on bad habits, but it is not the same organic "good" feeling I would experience after acting on a good habit.

Intentionality serves a bold purpose in committing to a habit because there is a change in someone's standard lifestyle and a new commitment. Dr. Carlo DiClemente says, "Once you

---

29 Jeremy Dean, *Making Habits, Breaking Habits: Why We Do Things, Why We Don't, and How to Make Any Change Stick* (Massachusetts: Da Capo Press, 2013), 11–12, Google Books.

30 Ibid. 14-15.

choose to change, you accept responsibility for changing. This responsibility is the burden of commitment...it is an acknowledgement that you are the only one who is able to respond, speak, and act for yourself."[31] When I see someone else put in time in the gym with such integrity, I can only observe a gamut of emotions. However, nobody in the gym knows the purpose behind this person's work ethic other than the person himself. He set an intention to follow a gym routine. The first couple of days and weeks may have taken some contemplative thoughts and adjustments. However, his commitment propelled an automatic mental approach in attacking whatever workout he sets for himself.

Through the principle of good habits, I can carry the lessons of a meaningful endeavor to be proactive on another goal, involving a completely different skillset. To be proactive does not mean I expect to power through an everyday task with no mental trance. Instead, it means I will develop and harness the right skills in this new habit to widen my perspective and focus on persistence. It means I will work smartly toward a definite chief aim, rather than simply work hard aimlessly. As Aristotle once said, "We are what we repeatedly do. Excellence, therefore, is not an act, but a habit."

Life is short. It is always worth the risk of taking on a new habit. Even though it may feel intimidating to you at first, your persistent effort will achieve a complete resonance with it. Enthusiasm is a great weapon to get the momentum

---

31   James O. Prochaska, Carlo C. DiClemente, and John C. Norcross, *Changing for Good: A Revolutionary Six-Stage Program for Overcoming Bad Habits and Moving Your Life Positively Forward* (Harper Collins, 2010), 30-31, Google Books.

started. However, along the way, that enthusiasm will inevitably die. Once that occurs, there must be a sustainable presence along the process—a purpose.

The "Why" is everything because it creates a craving to persist through the habit regardless of what roadblocks are in the way. Day One of any habit is the most exciting because of the unknown levels of success ahead in the process. Even though the intensity of the process may diminish this form of excitement, a purpose will maintain the same level of excitement throughout the setbacks and wins. Every day is a Day One!

CHAPTER 2

TIME MANAGEMENT AND SINGLE-TASKING

———

"Time is more valuable than money. You can get more money, but you cannot get more time."

—JIM ROHN

TIME MANAGEMENT

TIME MANAGEMENT FOR GOALS

Habits are not simply performed whenever someone feels like following them. They follow a specific schedule. The schedule does not come to the person; instead, the wise person is intentional in making the schedule and setting his goals. Psychologist Peg Dawson says, "People with strong time management skills meet deadlines, arrive on time for appointments or meetings, and can judge how long it takes to do any task thrown at them."[32]

On the other hand, people with poor time management skills have an irrational approach to getting work done. If they are serious about their work, Dawson says, "People with weak time management skills tend to have a particularly hard time with time estimation. They routinely underestimate how long it takes to do something...."[33]

People with good time management skills can judge any task's length of time based on past proactive action and post analysis. They are proactive critical thinkers. Self-development author Brian Tracy says, "For you to maximize your time, to enjoy the greatest quantity and quality of riches and rewards, you need to take time regularly to think about your goals, especially when you're experiencing turbulence and rapid change."[34] There is a common mantra—"It is easier said than done." Once I begin to realize how hard a component is in a process and do what it takes to overcome it, I come to the realization that time truly is my worst enemy. Usually, very impactful tasks require intensive thought and trial and error. It is not a snap process which can be finished in the matter of minutes.

32 Peg Dawson and Richard Guare, *The Smart but Scattered Guide to Success: How to Use Your Brain's Executive Skills to Keep Up, Stay Calm, and Get Organized at Work and at Home* (New York: The Guilford Press, 2016), 24–26, Google Books.

33 Ibid.

34 Brian Tracy, *Master Your Time, Master Your Life: The Breakthrough System to Get More Results, Faster, in Every Area of Your Life* (New York: Penguin Random House, 2016), 14–16, Google Books.

It is folly to think we live forever. Similarly, from a daily standpoint, it is folly to think our goals have feelings for us and give us more than a twenty-four-hour day. When I want to start a new healthy habit, I need to be proactive in managing my time around my typical habits, since it will lessen my time throughout the day toward other activities.

Time management coach Elizabeth Grace Saunders says, "Since time is a finite resource, by definition, using more of it for one activity decreases the amount that you have for another. For instance, if you spend ten hours of your day at work, seven hours sleeping, and two hours commuting, you have exactly five hours left to fit in everything else from brushing our teeth to talking to your family to reading a book."[35]

There is no other way to work around it. I need to commit to a time frame for every activity, not just vaguely set this activity "for the afternoon" and another "for the evening." This leads to procrastination and a loss of proactivity. If I lose my focus during one session of work, then I have to be proactive to be more efficient the next day in the same time frame. Time will not do the work for me. It is measured by my actions.

TIME MANAGEMENT FOR RELAXATION
In regard to our goals, time management is not limited to the actions we are proactive about. Relaxation needs its time management as well. I may be going one hundred miles per

---

35   Elizabeth Grace Saunders, *The 3 Secrets to Effective Time Investment: Achieve More Success with Less Stress* (China: McGraw Hill Companies, 2013), 23–25, Google Books.

hour every single day of the week and burn out through a lack of self-awareness. Professor Jon Kabat-Zinn says, "Unawareness can keep us from being in touch with our own body, its signals and messages...and living in a chronic state of unawareness can cause us to miss much of what is most beautiful and meaningful in our lives."[36]

Time management must be balanced to obtain a quality proactive lifestyle. Life is always changing. Relationships come and go. New purposes are developed, and adjustments are necessary. Time management for relaxation can train the brain to stay calm in the midst of unprecedented events, and to not completely lose scope of one's lifelong intentional aspirations.

TIME MANAGEMENT FROM A HEALTHY PERSPECTIVE

Time management is not as simple as putting a specific number of hours down on a sheet of paper to do something. The time of day is important as well. If I studied for an exam from 4:00 p.m. to 6:00 p.m., then my proactivity efficiency would not necessarily be the same as my focus for studying from 1:00 a.m. to 3:00 a.m. There is a science between how our minds and bodies read time at different periods of the day.

Dr. Satchin Panda refers to an internal clock we all have that innately senses the time of the day. From a morning perspective, he says that our internal clock prepares our body to wake up before actually waking up every morning. Panda adds, "It begins to shut down the production of the sleep

---

36 Jon Kabat-Zinn, *Full Catastrophe Living: Using the Wisdom of Your Body and Mind to Face Stress, Pain, and Illness* (New York: Bantam Books, 2013), 78–81, Google Books.

hormone melatonin from our pineal gland. Our breathing becomes slightly faster and our heartbeat picks up a few beats per minute as our blood pressure rises slightly."[37]

It is important to note this reset phase of the brain and body. I may have made a bad effort the previous day in achieving a task. However, if I manage my time to attack the same task the next morning, then I may have a more efficient proactive approach. Panda mentions the scientific explanation for this, saying, "Shortly after we open our eyes, the adrenal glands produce more of the stress hormone cortisol to help us rush through our morning routine."[38] If I can win the morning, I can win the day!

WHAT TIME GIVES YOU THE SPARK?

It is okay to play a trick on your brain and pick a time you know can get you in the groove. Personally, 8:30 a.m. and 8:30 p.m. are eye-popping times which give me that inspirational kick, considering my birthday is on August 30. As silly as it sounds, it can serve a deep purpose and bring out the best for one's intentions. This does not mean to say that I only begin my tasks at these times. However, they can provide some motivation if I realize the time during a hardship.

SINGLE-TASKING

Time management is one thing, but what you do within that time frame is another. I may feel very compelled to act on

---

37 Satchin Panda, *The Circadian Code: Lose Weight, Supercharge Your Energy, and Transform Your Health from Morning to Midnight* (New York: Penguin Random House, 2018), 24–27, Google Books.

38 Ibid.

something I planned to do; however, I can be sidetracked by interruptions and distractions. Therefore, single-tasking is the best method to give one hundred percent focus on the task in front of me. When I am proactive on something, there must be a chief aim and meaningful effort, as opposed to arbitrarily going through the motions with fragmented attention.

I obtained the best definition of single-tasking from a reading by Georgetown professor Cal Newport. He says, "To produce at your peak level you need to work for extended periods with full concentration on a single task free from distraction.... If you're not comfortable going deep for extended periods of time, it'll be difficult to get your performance to the peak levels of quality and quantity increasingly necessary to thrive professionally."[39]

In regards to single-tasking, the prefrontal cortex is the prime part of the brain. Professor Andrey Vyshedskiy defines the prefrontal cortex as being "responsible for executive functions, which includes planning complex cognitive behavior."[40] Scientists at the Institut national de la santé et de la recherche médicale (Inserm) in Paris once did a study where they had participants complete two tasks at the same time while undergoing functional magnetic resonance imaging (fMRI). The data showed that "the brain splits in half and causes us to forget details and make three times more mistakes when given two simultaneous goals."[41]

---

39   Cal Newport, *Deep Work: Rules for Focused Success in a Distracted World* (New York: Hachette Book Group, 2016), 36–39, Google Books.

40   Andrey Vyshedskiy, *On the Origin of the Human Mind* (MobileReference, 2014), 228–229, Google Books.

41   "To Multitask or Not to Multitask," USCDornsife, accessed September 5, 2020.

This led to the discovery that "working on a single task means both sides of the prefrontal cortex are working together in harmony" and "adding another task forces the left and right sides of the brain to work independently."[42] Even though it may be an irrational claim to say I can put the same effort solely into a task as I do halfheartedly, science has valid research to refute such a claim.

CAVEATS OF SINGLE-TASKING

Professor Adam Gazzaley refers to two caveats in single-tasking both of which can be internal or external: interruptions and distractions. Gazzaley defines the difference between the two concepts, saying, "Distractions are pieces of goal-irrelevant information that we either encounter in our external surroundings or generate internally within our own minds.... The difference from distractions is that interruptions happen when you make a decision to concurrently engage in more than one task at the same time, and even if you attempt to switch rapidly between them."[43]

I do not have control over my internal or external distractions. However, I must push through my intentions to finish what I started without voluntarily interrupting myself.

I struggle with a common interruption: the final product of a process. There are steps and times to achieve something. The vision of the product is great. However, single-tasking

42 Ibid.
43 Larry D. Rosen and Adam Gazzaley, *The Distracted Mind: Ancient Brains in a High-Tech World* (Massachusetts: The MIT Press, 2016), 22–24, Google Books.

puts an efficient effort solely into the current step in order to take the right step forward toward that product.

Present Moment Functioning expert Thomas M. Sterner says, "...when your mind is only on the finished product, not only do you feel frustrated in every second that you have not met that goal...you view each mistake as a barrier, something delaying you from realizing your goal and experiencing the joy that reaching that goal is going to give you."[44]

Intentionality is internal and the product is external. When I reach the end goal, I reflect on the process more than the product because the process is what made the product possible. To me, this realization begs the question: "How many more intentions do I have to contribute to my life's aspirations?"

Single-tasking gives a less stressful approach to efficient work because there are no other factors to react to. From a finished product standpoint, Sterner says, "When you shift your goal from the product you are trying to achieve to the process of achieving it...all pressure drops away."[45]

I believe the same applies to the external distractions I have in the moment of the process. I get deluded into thinking all my different thoughts must be acknowledged—as if the mental chaos is valuable work. However, the truth is

---

44 Thomas M. Sterner, *The Practicing Mind: Bringing Discipline and Focus into Your Life* (California: New World Library, 2012), 40–43, Google Books.

45 Thomas M. Sterner, *The Practicing Mind: Bringing Discipline and Focus into Your Life* (California: New World Library, 2012), 40–43, Google Books.

simple: intentionality gives undivided attention to one task at a time under the scheduled time frame. Proactivity is a full commitment.

THE MYTH OF MULTITASKING

Multitasking does not exist. You cannot do more than one thing at a time, even if it feels that way. Author Devora Zack references Stanford University neuroscientist Dr. Eyal Ophir on his perspective of this concept, saying, "Humans don't really multitask, we task-switch...switching very quickly between tasks."[46] She also notes Massachusetts Institute of Technology's Dr. Earl Miller's perspective: "You cannot focus on one task while doing another. That's because of what's called interference between the two tasks."[47]

Someone may refute this claim by asking how someone can chew gum and walk at the same time. Such casual actions are not built from proactive intentions. Zack says, "Activities that require virtually no conscious effort can be performed in conjunction with primary tasks and do not fall in the bandwidth of multitasking. "Simple" tasks are automated, low-level functions, including rote activities that do not require concentration."[48]

Cal Newport defines single-tasking somewhere along the lines of "deep work." Zack's "simple tasks" are what Newport describes as "shallow work:" "Noncognitively demanding,

---

46 Devora Zack, *Singletasking: Get More Done—One Thing at a Time* (California: Berrett-Koehler Publishers, 2015), 25–26, Google Books.

47 Ibid.

48 Ibid.

logistical-style tasks, often performed while distracted. These efforts tend to not create much new value in the world and are easy to replicate."[49]

On the other hand, intentional actions are so powerful because they are directed toward a creation which the pro-active person wants internally. Therefore, they require concentration. Task-switching will degrade one's focus.

EVERY MINUTE COUNTS

Time management is important because time is precious. Therefore, single-tasking is important because losing focus for one minute does two things: it loses the one minute which can give us that extra edge, and it also diverts our full focus away from our initial train of thought. In Chapter One, I noted that habits are developed and not instantaneously innate from the start. Single-tasking is a good way to initiate a new habit because it will feed into the basal ganglia much faster than through the "task-switching" procedure, which provides inconsistent information to the brain.

Emma Seppala, PhD, notes that it is not inherently bad to focus on getting things done, but does stress the importance of single-tasking. She says, "Constantly focusing on the next thing ironically ends up keeping you from the very success you are chasing. When everyone embraces the view that each minute is an opportunity to accomplish more and move ahead, you get caught up in this perspective and don't stop

---

49   Cal Newport, *Deep Work: Rules for Focused Success in a Distracted World* (New York: Hachette Book Group, 2016), 190-192, Google Books.

to question whether it's working for you."[50] The power of "now" is essential in single-tasking since it relates to focusing in the present moment. Proactivity involves doing what is right now for a better future.

In retrospect, I deluded myself into thinking that past good progress was due to serendipity. However, the feeling that was present in the process was normal and disciplined. We are all human beings. With proactivity comes a mature responsibility to be realistic and focus on one meaningful task at a time. Nobody is superhuman enough to put one hundred percent effort into two tasks at once. Time management involves doing one task, as opposed to two tasks, within a certain time frame.

50 Emma Seppala, *The Happiness Track: How to Apply the Science of Happiness to Accelerate Your Success* (San Francisco: HarperOne, 2016), 11–12, Google Books.

CHAPTER 3

SELF-CONTROL

"What it lies in our power to do, it lies in our power not to do."

—ARISTOTLE

SELF-CONTROL

In a proactive journey, a big principle to harness is self-control. In any rigorous endeavor, comfort and struggle cannot coexist. It is easy to lie on the couch and think of accomplishing a good feat in a swimming race: "I will manage my time to get me there." However, the habit to train nine sessions a week to get there is not so comfortable a thought. So, when the process begins, I am the most vulnerable to comfortable escapes. Even as the journey progresses, it is inevitable that comfort will always be a temptation.

Psychologist Walter Mischel is well-known for conducting a self-control experiment, known as the Marshmallow Test, on preschoolers at Stanford University's Bing Nursery School. He explains, "My students and I gave the children a choice between one reward (for example, one marshmallow) that they could have immediately, and a larger reward (two marshmallows) for which they would have to wait, alone, for up to twenty minutes."[51]

Proactivity can help delay instant gratification. I define it as being prudent when it comes to potential expedient temptations. If a child sees the marshmallow, they will want to eat it. Self-control plays a role in that the want for a future goal outweighs the want for an immediate pleasure. Mischel stayed in touch with the children and checked in with them again when they were in high school.

The children that had delayed eating the marshmallow had higher SAT scores and grades. Mischel says, "At ages twenty-seven to thirty-two, those who had waited longer during the Marshmallow Test in preschool had a lower body mass index and a better sense of self-worth, pursued their goals more effectively, and coped more adaptively with frustration and stress."[52] Self-control brings a special characteristic to proactivity: the power to say "no."

There is a common mantra: "When I am weak, I am strong." What this means to me is that when I am resisting temptation, I may feel "weak." However, I imagine a filled receptacle being emptied out and filled with new items, symbolizing strength. There is an equilibrium aspect to this. When I feel "strong" in feeding into my temptation, I am left feeling weak later. It is amazing how one subtle moment of strength can save you one thousand emotions of regret.

---

51 Walter Mischel, *The Marshmallow Test: Mastering Self-Control* (Little Brown Spark, 2014), 5–7, Google Books.

52 Ibid.

Author Lee Oberparleiter has worked as a teacher for over forty-five years and has developed many innovate ideas and techniques to use in instruction in Brain-Compatible teaching and learning. He describes the differences between two learning systems that exist in our brains: our rational thinking part—Learning System #2—and our irrational thinking part—Learning System #1. He says that Learning System #1 is the brain's primary learning system and "is triggered by the amygdala, the emotional trigger of the limbic system."[53] On the other hand, he says Learning System #2, which includes the prefrontal cortex (PFC), is the "last to become fully mature and develop, which places it at a disadvantage when interacting with the other emotional learning system circuit."[54]

If I act with intention and my internal purpose, my prefrontal cortex can take over the more potent limbic system's short-term desires. Oberparleiter describes "thinking" as the strength which the PFC has over the limbic system: "We need to think internally rather than reactively emote."[55] Thinking involves planning ahead and using memory and self-control to be proactive for the long term. Oberparleiter says, "The primary strength of (System #2) is that it can think with language and process experience not only in the immediate here and now, but it can actively process immediate experience into abstractions of the past and future. Then it can use those abstractions held in the mind (what we call working memory) to think with and to plan a future behavior."[56]

53 Lee Oberparleiter, *The Role of Emotion and Reflection of Student Achievement* (Indiana: AuthorHouse, 2011), 24–26, Google Books.

54 Ibid. 26–28.

55 Ibid. 26–28.

56 Ibid. 28–29.

An adult would not be as reluctant as a child in giving up temporary pleasure because an adult has matured and learned to wait. Self-control shows maturity and is what creates balance in the proactive lifestyle. It is what separates greatness, or high achievements, from mediocrity. Greatness is intentional in that it stems from internal thinking. This is a proactive challenge due to the potency of the limbic system.

If I am intent on doing something, then I have to be willing to overcome my primitive impulses with a proactive purpose. Constant temptations, if handled poorly, can lead to chaos. Jordan Peterson says, "Meaning is the ultimate balance between, on the one hand, the chaos of transformation and possibility, and on the other, the discipline of pristine order, whose purpose is to produce out of the attendant chaos a new order that will be even more immaculate, and capable of bringing forth a still more balanced and productive chaos and order."[57] Every intention has a purpose or meaning. Self-control brings order to the chaos.

Stanford psychologist Kelly McGonigal has a concept of the "I will, I won't, I want" approach to self-control. She says, ""I will" and "I won't" power are the two sides of self-control, but they alone don't constitute willpower. To say no when you need to say no, and yes when you need to say yes, you need a third power: the ability to remember what you really want."[58] Intentionality starts with the "want" for some-

---

57 Jordan Peterson, *12 Rules for Life: An Antidote to Chaos* (Toronto: Random House Canada, 2018), 231–233, Google Books.

58 Kelly McGonigal, *The Willpower Instinct: How Self-Control Works, Why It Matters, and What You Can Do to Get More of It* (New York: Penguin Group, 2012), 9–10, Google Books.

thing. It makes me think of why I began a good journey: : a rewarding future. The "I will" and "I won't" power focus on the present moment of temptation without necessarily connecting with my long-term ideas.

Cal Newport quotes psychologist Roy F. Baumeister on willpower: "You have a finite amount of willpower that becomes depleted as you use it."[59] Just like proactivity, willpower is an exercise. However, it can be very difficult on a daily basis to fight pleasurable temptations. In a way, I can trick my brain's desires to maintain focus on my aspirations. Newport has a clever insight, saying, "The key to developing a deep work habit is to move beyond good intentions and add routines and rituals to your working life designed to minimize the amount of your limited willpower necessary to transition into and maintain a state of unbroken concentration."[60] I want to develop new routines at a certain time of day when I feel most vulnerable to a certain pleasure. This will help me stay focused and not give in to more pleasurable activities.

Author Roman Gelperin notes an interesting perspective on pleasure, saying that the "pleasure unconscious does not just seek pleasure, but seeks to increase pleasure."[61] Pleasure, therefore, is relative. Gelperin supports this with an example of comparing someone playing a video game (pleasurable activity) to listening to music while doing homework (less

---

59   Cal Newport, *Deep Work: Rules for Focused Success in a Distracted World* (New York: Hachette Book Group, 2016), 82–84, Google Books.

60   Ibid.

61   Roman Gelperin, *Addiction, Procrastination, and Laziness: A Proactive Guide to the Psychology of Motivation* (Roman Gelperin, 2017), 26–27, Google Books.

pleasurable activity). He says that "this constitutes a decrease in pleasure, and the modus operandi of the pleasure unconscious makes the person extremely averse to such a change."[62]

As I mentioned in the previous chapter: "Win the morning, win the day!" If I start the day with a challenging or neutral task, then I am training my brain to overcome any unprecedented pleasing temptations throughout the day. For example, a cold shower creates a sense of discomfort, but after that cold shower, my mind has such a high level of willpower that my typical temptations seem suppressed. Self-control is an important exercise for a robust mindset.

MOUNTAINS MINDSET

On my journey toward my goals, I understand I am always susceptible to the trap of comfort. Personally, I will start the day with a hard workout and cold shower, or activities I hate. To keep this serious mindset, I meditate on how I overcame the temptation to sleep in and take a hot shower. This is a trick which helps me boost my confidence to overcome more comfortable pleasures in the course of my serious duties.

My journey is similar to a series of mountains. I want to climb each mountain upward with integrity and self-control as opposed to finding the shortcuts to avoid any struggle. The struggles I experience will help me achieve my goal of reaching the peak of the mountain and will also provide me the strength for the next climb. I always tell myself, "Even if I do not reach the top of the mountain today, despite my

---

62   Ibid.

self-control, I am well-assured that I will go harder tomorrow and once again defeat comfortable temptations."

LACK OF SELF-CONTROL

If I lack self-control and give in to cheap pleasures, then I may develop a bad habit. Dr. Robert Lustig is a Professor Emeritus of Pediatrics at the University of California, San Francisco, who has studied the danger of an excessive amount of the "reward" neurotransmitter, dopamine. He explains the fundamentals of dopamine, saying, "...dopamine excites neurons...and neurons when they're excited too much, tend to die. So, the neuron has a defensive mechanism against that... it reduces the number of receptors that are available to be stimulated in an attempt to mitigate the damage."[63]

Self-control is an important exercise to avoid superfluously seeking a dopamine rush. Lustig explains, "You get a hit, you get a rush, the receptors go down. Next time, you need a bigger hit to get the same rush because there are fewer receptors to occupy. And you need a bigger hit, and a bigger hit, until finally taking a huge hit to get nothing. That's called tolerance. And then when the neurons start to die, that's called addiction."[64] Serotonin, on the other hand, is another chemical the brain releases. Dr. Lustig relates serotonin to happiness instead of pleasure, stating its neuron's function: "It inhibits its receptor to provide contentment...so you can't overdose the serotonin neuron."[65]

---

63 Robert Lustig, "The Hacking of the American Mind with Dr. Robert Lustig," filmed September 2017 at University of California, video, 32:42.
64 Ibid.
65 Ibid.

Based on Lustig's information, I ideally want a state of contentment, as it keeps me in the present moment and inhibits any emotional drive for pleasure. The cheap pleasures of the world will control me if am not cognizant of my own control. Enough pleasure is enough. That is self-control. Too much pleasure damages my ability to control my actions, hence why I have my intentions.

THE ROCKY VS. ROSY ROAD

Whenever I am on the verge of giving in to a temporary comfort, I think of a bad spirit leading me down a rosy road. This road will only lead to self-destruction the more I travel on it, as opposed to making the proper sacrifices on the rocky road to achieve a higher end of success.

For example, I can wake up and easily desire the rosy road of taking a hot shower or eating a sugary treat because I envision it with pleasure. However, the lack of self-control in this act will lead me downhill toward a perpetual and unhealthy habit of acting on comfortable desires. I see myself as either progressing forward efficiently or losing control and speeding downhill.

SELF-CONTROL VS. LACK OF SELF-CONTROL

Proactivity can be confused with acting on our goals perpetually without any boundaries. Self-control sets boundaries but in a meaningful and conducive manner. A lack of self-control may have a confused meaning, moving forward 115 miles per hour despite giving into temporary comfort. Speed is one concept, but direction is another. A lack of self-control can disrupt our direction and set a bad trend. It is important to take that step back in times of temptation, and to stabilize our focus while maintaining an acceptable rate of speed toward our goals. Set those boundaries!

CHAPTER 4

FEARLESSNESS
AND MEDITATION

"Our deepest fear is not that we are inadequate. Our deepest fear is that we are powerful beyond measure. It is our light, not our darkness that most frightens us."

—MARIANNE WILLIAMSON

To be fearless we need to know more about fear itself. Just because someone is fearless does not mean he does not fear anything. In the previous chapter, I discussed self-control and pleasure. Pleasure is something we can find through external sources. On the other hand, fear is something we must let go of internally. Fear makes us stagnant. When I develop habits that help me move past my fear, I can look back on it later and see how the fear was irrational. As Franklin D. Roosevelt said, "The only thing we have to fear is fear itself."

AMYGDALA

Fear comes from the amygdala. Professor Catherine Pittman says, "When you're experiencing the fight, flight, or freeze response, the amygdala is in the driver's seat, and you're a passenger. That's why in emergency situations, you often feel as though you're observing yourself responding rather than consciously controlling your response."[66] When you act with intention, you are overriding the amygdala. Pittman explains that "the amygdala isn't just faster—it also has the neurological capability to override other brain processes."[67]

Since the amygdala has power over the PFC, my PFC may struggle with reasoning. Every time I am faced with a similar experience that I once reacted fearfully to, then I may feel confused as to why I am fearful and start a degrading trend of "freezing." Since the prefrontal cortex shuts down in fight-or-flight situations, my only proactive option is to evaluate these experiences in a future relaxed state of mind.

Pittman says that "evidence suggests that amygdala-based memory is longer lasting than cortex-based memory…the cortex is much more likely than the amygdala to forget information or have trouble retrieving it."[68] Hence, it is my duty to be proactive in knowing the crux of emotional resistance.

Dr. Michael Davis, a psychiatrist at Yale University School of Medicine, did an experiment placing a mouse—with an

---

66 Catherine M. Pittman and Elizabeth M. Karle, *Rewire Your Anxious Brain: How to Use the Neuroscience of Fear to End Anxiety, Panic, and Worry* (California: New Harbinger Publications, 2015), 39–41, Google Books.
67 Ibid. 41–43.
68 Ibid. 49–51.

original wound and a useless amygdala—with a cat in a confined space. He explained the mouse's action, saying, "A mouse with such a condition walked slowly toward the cat and began to lick its ear...a mouse with a normal condition had never shown such behaviour."[69]

The difference between this mouse's actions and a normal conditioned mouse's actions are reflected in the absence or presence of the amygdala. Based on this, it is important to understand the significance of the amygdala's neuroscience because it is the center of our fears. Our fears should not induce us into putting a weak label on ourselves; they are a nature of the brain. However, we can overcome them by simply taking the initiative in facing them!

Marc Dingman, PhD, has a concept known as "fear conditioning." He explains a fear experiment in which a rat would hear a neutral beeping tone and would afterwards give the rat a mild electric shock. After this experience, the rat would show signs of fear every time the beeping tone sounded, whether there was a shock or not. Dingman connects the word "fear" to the word "conditioning," explaining that "conditioning involves learning to make an association between two things that previously didn't have a strong connection in the mind."[70] My conscious mind creates my fears, but I must harness my memory to let go of what caused them.

---

69 Desh Subba, *Philosophy of Fearism: Life is Conducted, Directed and Controlled by the Fear* (Desh Subba, 2014), 15--17, Google Books.

70 Marc Dingman, *Your Brain, Explained: What Neuroscience Reveals about Your Brain and its Quirks* (UK: Nicholas Brealey Publishing, 2019), 26–28, Google Books.

DISCOMFORT VS. DISTRESS

Jennice Vilhauer, PhD, says, "When you first step outside your comfort zone, you will likely experience fear, which is very normal…. Fear alerts us to possible danger and tells us to prepare for it."[71] I need to first accept fear and realize it is a base for my success journey. There is no other way around it. The question is: "How will I harness my fear?"

In regard to discomfort, Vilhauer says, "You may feel uncomfortable, but you are still really looking forward to where you are going."[72] For distress, she says, "The negative feelings are overwhelming you, and you can't focus on your desired goal."[73] I may have fears which trace back over a decade ago, I may never know the source of my fears, but I can channel through discomfort to produce control over them.

A friend once told me, "Pay now or pay later." Fear can set limits on us, which may result in self-doubt. The longer this lingers, the more ground we have to make up in the future, which creates even more fear. It is better to go through the discomfort to "pay now" than to go through the distress of having to "pay later." This boosts confidence and experience, as well as mitigates overthinking.

I can delude myself into thinking of the "magical date" I can finally act on something. However, "now" is the best time to face a fear. One technique is to minimize the number of

---

71 Jennice Vilhauer, *Think Forward to Thrive: How to Use the Mind's Power of Anticipation to Transcend Your Past and Transform Your Life* (California: New World Library, 2014), 31---33, Google Books.

72 Ibid. 33–35.

73 Ibid. 33–35.

expectations you have for a certain task. This leads to a feeling of liberation and healthy risk, as if you have nothing to lose. You can also write down your goals and read them out loud. There is beauty behind this because the words are in your own handwriting and were thoroughly written.

Third, it is key to "just flow" rather than "force" oneself to do something. Force creates resistance since there is a reluctant aspect to having to try to do something one has no passion for. Flowing emits a natural and fearless action to chase after a goal, whether it results in a success or failure. This does not imply that one is not trying, but that one is taking the intention to explore a new opportunity.

FEARLESSNESS

If I act with intention, fear should not stop me. If I let fear stop me, I am not acting with intention. It would hurt to leave this planet without exploring as many personal intentions to bring the best out in me. Just the thought of death propels me to be proactive in satisfying my soul, which is eternal.

Vietnamese Buddhist Zen Master Thich Nhat Hanh says, "To really be free of fear, we must look deeply into the ultimate dimension to see our true nature of no-birth and no-death.... When we understand that we are more than our physical bodies, that we didn't come from nothingness and will not disappear into nothingness, we are liberated from fear."[74]

---

74 Thich Nhat Hanh, *Fear: Essential Wisdom for Getting Through the Storm* (Harper One Publishers, 2012), 5–7, Google Books.

Intentions come from within the heart and soul. I find such beauty in the idea that we do not have a physical portrayal of either aspect. It creates wonder and joy in the unknown. This can be a good motivator in uplifting the heart and soul's well-being and embracing their presences despite our fear. Even though we may not see how our heart and soul physically reacts to our intense passions, the best way we can sense it is through the outcomes of our intentions.

I see the two sides of our minds in a constant battle with themselves. There is the bad side which induces you into thinking you are not worth achieving a certain accolade, and that may bring up memories of past failures. And then the other side gives a sanguine approach to being proactive.

Sometimes I struggle understanding why I do not act upon my goals. It is important to note that there may be some background in the subconscious mind. Dr. Friedemann Schaub says, "A conflict between two subconscious parts often shows up as procrastination and inconsistent, even self-sabotaging behavior. You forge one step forward and retreat two steps back; you come up with promising ideas and impactful commitments, but then find yourself never following through."[75]

I believe there is fear related to procrastination. Perhaps I am fearful that my efforts will prove futile. If I ignored this fear, then a negative mental voice would only grow louder and ask me, "So, you are not going to be proactive about it and accept it?" Schaub explains the ignorance of fear, saying

75 Friedemann Schaub, *The Fear and Anxiety Solution: Guided Practices for Healing and Empowerment with Your Subconscious Mind* (Colorado: Sounds True, 2012), 40, Google Books.

that "by eliminating a part of yourself, even if that part is negative…you would actually cause a fragmentation of your subconscious mind, which is the opposite of healing and wholeness…the stronger and more obnoxious it seemed to become…it was impossible for you to mute its voice and feelings."[76] When something feels so important to chase after, we need to be proactive to create a map to carve the path to achieve it regardless of the fears, doubts, and odds. That loud haunting sound will only lead to a perpetual state of regret. A scary process may cause us to think superfluously of the regimen required to overcome it. But, ironically, it may take just a single big step to get its substance in the right perspective. For example, a fear to swim can be a constant issue in someone's head. However, the simple steps of jumping in and familiarizing one's self with the water can provide a major confidence boost to take the further steps necessary to overcome the fear of swimming.

Intentionality trumps insecurities by taking that first step in the process. Fear is not a physical monster that will destroy you. Imagine fear as a lightweight chair that has a string attached to your ankle. You can still move from one place to another, despite the "fear" lingering on your ankle. You can either move, or you can give more power to the chair, despite its stagnant and inferior status to you. Try, just try.

The big question should be: "How am I going to be proactive if this scenario takes place?" Our intentions are internal, and if we focus on ourselves, then we can be proactive

---

76 Friedemann Schaub, *The Fear and Anxiety Solution: Guided Practices for Healing and Empowerment with Your Subconscious Mind* (Colorado: Sounds True, 2012), 40, Google Books.

in dealing with our fears to the best of our abilities. I may have an assignment due later in the week and fear that an upcoming storm may cut my house's electricity. However, I can be proactive in finishing the paper before the week's end, or at least brainstorm my ideas in advance. Giving into fear will lead to inactivity.

Fearlessness is doing what needs to be done despite the odds being against me. It is better to just "not think" regarding the analysis of our emotions. David Corbonell, PhD, stresses the waste of energy in convincing one's self that an external circumstance will not arrive. It is important to accept life the way it is and understand that we only have control over our intentions, not external circumstances.

Corbonell says, "You can recognize that it's very unlikely, but there's no way to prove to yourself that some calamity isn't going to happen tomorrow because just about anything, no matter how improbable, is possible if your rules of evidence are loose enough."[77] Nobody can predict when death will arrive, and we have no control over it. However, there is a "death" we can beat in life, which I refer to as inactivity. Risk-taking defines fearlessness. My intentions are risks. Life is a risk. Forget fear—the bad fear, that is.

To have a proactive lifestyle is to be proactive with the good fear. This good fear may create discomfort, but I view it as the fear of obtaining new knowledge. Philosopher René Descartes once said, "Knowledge without skepticism is impossible and

---

77   David A. Carbonell, *The Worry Trick: How Your Brain Tricks You into Expecting the Worst and What You Can Do About It* (California: New Harbinger Publications, 2016), 27–29, Google Books.

it can be possible only via skepticism. So, skepticism is useful for knowledge and truth."[78] Within every intention is a learning process. I obtain knowledge of matters I do not know of beforehand. Therefore, fear, through skepticism, can motivate a curious and proactive approach from me.

Moving forward in life, it is important to be proactive in acknowledging what fears other people share with us, or to acknowledge why a task possesses an ominous nature to us. In other words, I need to be cognizant of how I interpret external information. It adds to my knowledge, and a misinterpretation of it may lead to an irrational fear. Philosopher Desh Subba says, "Knowledge is consciousness, but consciousness is not knowledge. Everybody has consciousness, but knowledge about everything is not possible—fear starts with knowledge."[79] Prudence and open-mindedness can help promote facts and not fear.

MEDITATION

There is a special habit used to gain more consciousness and give control to the prefrontal cortex over the amygdala: meditation. When the amygdala initiates the fight-or-flight response, Dr. Susan Shumsky says that it "damages cells and shrinks the hippocampus...in contrast, meditation activates the prefrontal cortex, which reduces anxiety and trauma."[80]

---

78 Desh Subba, *Philosophy of Fearism: Life is Conducted, Directed and Controlled by the Fear* (Desh Subba, 2014), 15–17, Google Books.

79 Ibid. 62–65.

80 Susan Shumsky, *Awaken Your Third Eye: How Accessing Your Sixth Sense Can Help You Find Knowledge, Illumination, and Intuition* (New Jersey: The Career Press, 2015), 76–78, Google Books.

The hippocampus is part of the limbic system, which "regulates motivation, emotion, learning, and memory."[81] Meditation promotes intentionality and courage.

Shumsky says, "Brain scans show that meditators shrink their amygdala and increase their hippocampus. This reduces stress and increases emotional stability and the ability to live in the present."[82] Meditation fosters "a new beginning" for me after every session. The fears from the past and the fears of the future or the unknown do not exist during and shortly after this mindful practice. Only my intentions are clear.

Dr. Robert Puff says, "Fears and worries come when our minds are working, going from the past to the future, thinking about what has been and what could be. When we make our minds quiet and be in moment, fears and worries go away."[83]

This relates to my definition of proactivity: an efficient approach to chasing my aspirations. Speed is not as important as direction. It is unhealthy to move forward inconsistently or in the wrong direction. Meditation provides that rest stop to settle and revisit the direction I need to travel in order to maximize my best efforts.

81 Dr. Sanchari Sinha Dutta, "Hippocampus Functions," News Medical, accessed September 7, 2020.
82 Susan Shumsky, *Awaken Your Third Eye: How Accessing Your Sixth Sense Can Help You Find Knowledge, Illumination, and Intuition* (New Jersey: The Career Press, 2015), 74–76, Google Books.
83 Dr. Robert Puff, *Reflections on Meditation: A Guide for Beginners* (California: Ebookit.com, 2011), 14, Google Books.

The most important part of meditation is observing the breath. When we breathe, in general, we inhale oxygen, which our brains need to function efficiently. Annellen M. Simpkins, PhD, says, "Through evolution, human beings developed a more sophisticated nervous system for providing the amount of oxygen needed to sustain a large brain. Thus, our respiratory system prompted the development of advanced abilities for orienting, paying attention, and regulating emotions."[84] Through meditation, I am attaching myself to what is necessary for my cognitive abilities: a clear mind and oxygen. To feel rejuvenated, nothing else matters but this.

Another component of meditation is stillness. This form of stillness is not sloth, but a prudent step back to think realistically and ambitiously. Author Deepak Chopra says, "Stillness alone is the potentiality for creativity; movement alone is creativity restricted to a certain aspect of expression. But the combination...enables you to unleash your creativity in all directions—wherever the power of your attention takes you."[85] This relates to balancing fear with reason.

Meditation is the main weapon against fear. I should not look at meditation as an escape or something to get better at; rather, it is an exercise to give me the edge on my consciousness of reality. Meditation expert Emily Fletcher has a

---

84 Annellen M. Simpkins and C. Alexander Simpkins, *Meditation and Yoga in Psychotherapy: Techniques for Clinical Practice* (New Jersey: John Wiley & Sons, 2011), 45–47, Google Books.

85 Deepak Chopra, *The Seven Spiritual Laws of Success: A Practical Guide to the Fulfillment of Your Dreams* (California: Amber-Allen Publishing, 1994), 19–22, Google Books.

concept of the three M's of meditation. She explains, "Mindfulness helps you deal with stress in the present; meditation gets rid of stress from the past; and manifesting helps you clarify your dreams for the future."[86]

One strong intention I place in meditation is gratitude. I have to be mindful of my current stresses and gauge them against other people's more intense issues. Yes, I do have a right to be concerned about my problems, but I must instill confidence in myself that they can be overcome, and that I do not possess others' unfortunate circumstances. Things could be much worse.

My worries of the past may linger on and blind me to the current gifts I hold. This is where meditation conquers these past fears. I can manifest a game plan: "I feel so grateful for my blessings. So, am I going to let fear hold me back from the opportunities I have which others would die for?"

This is what meditation does: clears the mind in the present, leaves the past behind, and creates a new vision. I wrongly tend to view meditation as a waste of time during which I could be actively doing something toward my goals. However, meditation actually centralizes my mind with a real and raw focus in an appropriate time-out. Just as athletes take time-outs in games to recover energy, my mind needs intentional recovery to let go of fear and plan with faith.

---

86 Emily Fletcher, *Stress Less, Accomplish More: Meditation for Extraordinary Performance* (HarperCollinsPublishers, 2019), 24–26, Google Books.

FOUR STEPS OF MEDITATION TO CONQUER FEAR

Whether it was before a big swim season, months of preparation for the GMAT, or a new academic year, I would have some fear regarding which direction my training would go. There are many types of fears to have, such as the fear of losing an opportunity, fear regarding physical and mental health, or fear of failing. As a perfectionist, I had a fear of failing. So how do I overcome it?

Irony can be a beautiful aspect. If someone does the opposite of what is right, then things will go wrong. However, there is a good irony. Since I had a consistent fear of failing, I told myself that I would feel the opposite and be willing to fail. The more stones thrown at me in the process would give me more opportunities to learn and build a castle with them. Here is a four-step process I personally like to follow to avoid irrational fear as someone with a perfectionist mentality:

- Maximize direction and minimize speed: Build the speed in the beginning of any process in a prudent manner and identify the early mistakes to learn from for future reference. In this way, my fears become my friends.
- Block out the outside world, close your eyes tight, and meditate: This will make you more cognizant of your current place in the moment and will provide laser focus to go after anything you want, despite your fears.
- Open your eyes and trust the big ambitions you meditated over, no matter how superfluous they may be.
- Steps One, Two, and Three will produce the "Forget It" mentality to go all in and plow through your fears!

Fears are internal, and meditation helps mitigate our internal stresses. As irrational as our fears are, we should meditate boldly to balance both the rational and irrational. Take the proactive approach to the four steps instead of a nonchalant style of reactivity in the midst of fears and failures.

CHAPTER 5

HEALTH (WATER AND NUTRITION, SLEEP, EXERCISE)

"It is health that is real wealth and not pieces of gold and silver."

−MAHATMA GANDHI

Staying healthy is an important part of accomplishing my goals. Good physical health correlates well with optimal brain functioning. In this chapter, I will touch base on nutrition, sleep, and exercise. Proactivity is more than just mental power. Physical well-being is a conducive supplement to mental health.

WATER

Water is the necessity of life and is the base for a proactive lifestyle. Dr. Lisa Mosconi says, "Water is indispensable for energy production—that's because it carries oxygen, which is needed for your working cells to breathe and burn sugar to produce energy. Water also plays a structural role, filling in the spaces between brain cells, and also helps to form proteins, absorb nutrients, and eliminate waste products."[87]

In the battle with our emotions and fears, water helps keep the mind sharp and energetic for the executive functions to follow through. On the other hand, a lack of water intake can lead to a dysfunctional mental focus. Mosconi says that dehydration "disrupts energy processes and causes loss of electrolytes…three to four percent decrease in water intake will almost immediately affect the brain's fluid balance, causing a number of issues like fatigue, brain fog, reduced energy, headaches, and mood swings…"[88]

A weak body causes a weak mind. Mosconi references an experiment conducted by researchers from the UK regarding water's effect on cognitive performance and mood, where some participants ate only a cereal bar and the rest ate a cereal bar along with drinking water. Afterwards, all participants had to complete a series of mental tests. Mosconi says that "those who drank around three cups of water just before completing the tests showed significantly faster reaction times compared with those who did not drink any water."[89] The best benefit we can add to our intentions every morning is to start with a fresh glass of water. Win the morning, win the day!

---

87 Lisa Mosconi, *Brain Food: The Surprising Science of Eating for Cognitive Power* (New York: Penguin Random House, 2018), 43–45, Google Books.

88 Ibid.

89 Ibid.

NUTRITION

Good nutrition is necessary for brain health. *The British Journal of Psychiatry* once published a large study that stated "eating processed foods...increased the risk of depression by about sixty percent. Eating a whole-food diet...decreased the risk of depression by about twenty-six percent."[90] Regardless of how intentional I am toward a goal, I need to be cognizant of my eating habits.

Dr. Drew Ramsey describes his "Three-Point Plan for Happiness": cognitive functioning, emotional regulation, and anxiety. He is describing three things that need to be controlled to achieve happiness. You need clear and focused attention, an ability to plan, and a way to regulate your emotions.

If I want to exercise self-control and fearlessness on my intentional journey, then good nutrition is the fuel to get the engine started. Ramsey refers to a special protein in the brain known as the brain-derived neurotrophic factor (BDNF), which is responsible for our receptors, emotions, and cognitive skills.

He says, "Reduce BDNF levels in the brain and you feel blue, forget things, and can't learn. Increase BDNF and brain areas central to thinking and feeling look healthy and robust, with their neurons making thousands of connections."[91] Our brains have neuroplasticity (the ability of neural networks in the brain to change through growth and reorganization),

---

90 Drew Ramsey and Tyler Graham, *The Happiness Diet: A Nutritional Prescription for a Sharp Brain, Balanced Mood, and Lean, Energized Body* (Rodale Books, 2012), 23–24, Google Books.

91 Ibid. 27–29.

and our food choices determine how we manage our cognitive abilities. Ramsey says, "Eat more processed, high sugar foods and BDNF levels go down. Eat foods with plenty of folate, vitamin B12, omega-3 and your BDNF levels go up."[92]

My brain is like a muscle. If I train my legs to run almost every day, I will develop a more efficient stride. Similarly, if I feed my brain the right nutrition regularly, I can improve my proactivity in getting my work done. One cheat meal, just like one bad workout, per week will not ruin my overall mental performance.

There is a major stress hormone in the body called cortisol. Dr. Jonny Bowden says that "the release of cortisol sets off a chain reaction that can harm both brain and body if cortisol levels become too high for sustained periods of time and therefore unmanageable…if you eat a lot of nutrient poor carbohydrates…and bad fats, and at the same time you don't eat enough clean protein, smart fat, and healthy fiber, your cortisol machinery gets all screwed up."[93] Fast food may appeal to my comfort zone if I get stressed at one time. However, expediency, through a poor diet, will only lead to more stress and inactivity for my intentions.

SLEEP

A proactive lifestyle needs a reset button to refuel our limited energetic abilities. Sleep is a major base for energy restoration and rejuvenation to continue striving for our aspirations. Dr.

---

92   Ibid.

93   Steven Masley and Jonny Bowden, *Smart Fat: Eat More Fat. Lose More Weight. Get Healthy Now.* (Harper Collins, 2016), 18–20, Google Books.

Marc Dingman explains how sleep recovers the demand for our mindful activities during the day, saying, "We use amino acids to synthesize proteins, adenosine triphosphate for energy, glucose to make more ATP, and so on...during sleep, your body (and even more so your brain) can take a break from the incessant demand for energy and focus on replenishing depleted stores of these essential substances."[94]

Sleep helps provide a fresh start against all restrictions which impede us from using the right judgment against our emotions and fears. Dr. John B. Arden says that "sleep deprivation has been shown to compromise attention, new learning, and memory."[95] He adds that there are new neurons which grow in the part of the brain involved with memory—the hippocampus—and "studies have shown that sleep deprivation impairs the ability of these stem cells to grow and become new neurons."[96]

I look at a sleep deprived body like a wagon with no wheels. It can move, but it takes a lot of mental and physical chaos to steer it in the right direction and pick up speed. Author Shawn Stevenson refers to an explanation from a researcher's study that states how "simultaneously, your brain cells are reduced in size by about sixty percent while you're asleep to make waste removal even more efficient." This significant decrease indicates the power of sleep on restoration of

94 Marc Dingman, *Your Brain, Explained: What Neuroscience Reveals about Your Brain and its Quirks* (Massachusetts: Nicholas Breasley Publishing, 2019), 77–79, Google Books.

95 John B. Arden, *Rewire Your Brain: Think Your Way to a Better Life* (New Jersey: John Wiley & Sons, 2010), 130.

96 Ibid.

energy for the next day. Sleep, like proactivity, is an exercise in recovery.

It is important to know when you sleep best. Everyone is different in this respect. Dr. Matthew Walker mentions three types of sleepers: morning types, evening types, and the types of people who are in-between. He describes how morning types make up "about forty percent of the populace (and) they prefer to wake at or around dawn...and function optimally at this time of day."[97] Evening types make up about "thirty percent of the population. They naturally prefer going to bed late and subsequently wake up late the following morning, or even in the afternoon."[98] Walker says that "the remaining thirty percent of people lie somewhere in between morning and evening types, with a slight leaning toward eveningness."[99]

I tend to be an evening type, or a night owl. It takes a while for me to get warmed up in the morning because of my late-night habits. I feel that taking the proactive approach of getting out of bed early may shift my habit toward a morning type person because, perhaps, I may have a new intention I will only have time for in the morning.

Walker describes the night owl mentality by saying, "When a night owl is forced to wake up early, their prefrontal cortex remains in a disabled, "offline" state. Like a cold engine after an early-morning start, it takes a long time before it warms

---

97 Matthew Walker, *Why We Sleep: Unlocking the Power of Sleep and Dreams* (Simon and Schuster, 2017), 23-25, Google Books.

98 Ibid.

99 Ibid.

up to operating temperature, and before that will not function efficiently."[100]

Sleep helps reset our awareness for our purpose and promotes consistency in our intentions. Without it, we lose our logic. Author Arianna Huffington quotes Till Roenneberg, a professor at the Ludwig Maximilian University of Munich, describing sleep deprivation well: "Memory capacity is reduced. Social competence is reduced. Your entire performance is going to suffer. The way you make decisions changed."[101]

I need to maintain good memory to build on current ideas. I need a genuine reputation from my social circle by making logical decisions. Poor sleep can delude my thinking, and thus can make others think I have a diminished ability to think. Sleep is a crucial part of the proactive equation with action!

EXERCISE

Exercise helps reduce stress levels and provides a boost of confidence in tasks we would otherwise find overwhelming. Dr. Daniel G. Amen says that exercise "boosts blood flow, increases the brain's use of oxygen, and improves your brain's response to stress…and is one of the best ways to change your shape and improve your mood…."[102]

---

100 Ibid.

101 Arianna Huffington, *The Sleep Revolution: Transforming Your Life, One Night at a Time* (New York: Harmony, 2016), 36–39, Google Books.

102 Daniel G. Amen, *Change Your Brain, Change Your Body: Use Your Brain to Get and Keep the Body You Have Always Wanted* (New York: Harmony, 2010), 40–41, Google Books.

Overthinking and complacency lead to inactivity. Action and rhythm lead to progress. Kelly McGonigal says that regular exercise "remodels the physical structure of your brain to make you more repetitive to joy and social connection... during physical activity, muscles secrete hormones into your bloodstream that make your brain more resilient to stress... scientists called them 'hope molecules.'"[103]

Every time I leave the gym, I feel I can take on any task I felt resistant to prior to my workout. If I can get in a good quality workout, then I can apply that energy to any other intention I put my mind to. Intentionality is solely from our internal convictions. As weak as they may sound to others, they mean something genuine and purposeful to ourselves because only we can understand our own internal struggles. McGonigal says, "The psychical pastimes we are most drawn to seem uniquely devised to harness our individual strengths—the ability to persist, endure, learn, and grow—while simultaneously rousing our instincts to work together."[104]

Nobody else is doing the push-ups for me. After a great workout, I can accept the reality: "I created this, just like I can create my own future." McGonigal refers to experiments in the US and UK where active adults replaced exercise with inactivity. After two weeks, she says they became "more anxious, tired, and hostile.... When adults are randomly assigned to reduce their daily step count, eighty-eight percent become more depressed. Within one week of becoming

103 Kelly McGonigal, *The Joy of Movement: How Exercise Helps Us Find Happiness, Hope, Connection, and Courage* (New York: Penguin, 2019), 4–6, Google Books.
104 Ibid. 6–8.

more sedentary, they report a thirty-one percent decline in life satisfaction."[105]

These findings indicate that physical movement correlates with proactive movement. Any intention is an exercise, which requires persistence. Exercise has something known as the "runner's high" (a feeling of euphoria with less anxiety) after persistent effort. When I achieve this feeling, it makes me want to achieve the same feeling toward my intentions. McGonigal says, "The runner's high is the temporary reward that carries us to our bigger goals…you get to experience yourself as someone who digs in and keeps going when things get tough."[106] There is deliberate and internal action in exercise!

HEALTH

Nutrition, sleep, and exercise all have similar effects on our proactive lifestyles. They contribute to energy, optimism, and internal confidence that lead us to function and persist. Early proactivity to our self-care will set our minds right and let us know what is right from wrong before it becomes a hard habit to break in the future. Self-care is an everyday exercise!

---

105 Ibid. 14–16.
106 Ibid. 23–25.

CHAPTER 6

IMAGINATION

"The man who has no imagination has no wings."

—MUHAMMAD ALI

IMAGINATION: OUR PERSONAL CREATIONS

Imagination is the ability to harness our old and current ideas to create something new, whether it be ideas or energy. With my imagination, I am in my own world inside my head, and nobody else can completely understand my intentions. The only reality which exists at every moment is the present moment. The past no longer exists but is placed as memories in our minds. On the other hand, the future is unknown. Proactivity is doing what it takes to get to the next level or to develop a new skill.

I must harness my current knowledge from the past in order to innovate a new self-identity. But, a new idea must be rational. To imagine I can teach an animal to speak English, to me, is irrational. However, to imagine myself hitting a one-mile personal record in six months is rational. I compare my imagination to a house construction map. I can gradually draw out what I define as an ideal house by using my imagination; that, however, is just the spark of the idea.

Proactivity is building on the drawn map. This requires a realistic approach of how the base of the house will start to reasonably support the second-floor architecture. I cannot act on my intentions without using my imagination because there would otherwise be no insight on my goal. I have to picture not only the end goal, but also, more importantly, the crucial steps needed to get there.

Imagination can help me have an encouraging conversation with myself: "I will get this part of the job done at this time, and I will breathe a sigh of relief after I completely finish what I set out for at the end of the day." In regards to new energy, I can use my imagination to harness a past negative experience or failure and propel myself to overcome my flaws, or I can harness a past success for the confidence in believing I can achieve a successful result again. Imagination is powerful!

In order to absorb new ideas, I need to be proactive in making more experiences; this will widen my gamut of imagination. Professor Javy Wong Galindo says, "Many creative texts that talk about inventors and artistic geniuses seem to point to serendipity and perseverance as a common underlying factor of their creative process…within this context, creativity appears to be the result of hard work, skill, and in some sense, luck."[107]

---

107 Javy W. Galindo, *The Power of Thinking Differently: An Imaginative Guide to Creativity, Change, and the Discovery of New* (California: Enlightened Hyene Press, 2009), 20–21, Google Books.

I may feel scared to fail as I act through my intentions, but good will always come out of it: new ideas for imagination. This is what makes proactivity very beneficial, no matter what the outcome may be. I sometimes wonder what unknown sources I get creative ideas from. The answer is the subconscious mind. I can only let my conscious mind accept these ideas for analysis. Galindo says that the unconscious mind "may in fact be more suited for creative insight than the conscious mind because it has no self-censorship and makes no judgments...ideas are free to recombine with others to form novel associations and unique patterns."[108] It is remarkable how I get new ideas when I'm not trying. Application is what makes the magic a reality!

Your intentions will always be internal. Your actions that are based on your intentions are external. This is exactly what my imagination is primed to do. Author Elizabeth Gilbert says, "A creative life is an amplified life...living in this manner—continually and stubbornly bringing forth the jewels that are hidden within you—is a fine art, in and of itself."[109]

When I have an unexpected idea, I question the validity of making it a reality. Nobody else can read the conversation I am having but me, which makes my intentions even more powerful. You earn your imagination and innovative thoughts by connecting the dots of your past. Anyone else will not fully understand your imagination because they were not in your shoes your whole life. What may resonate with you may sound like folly to others. This is why it is important

---

108 Ibid. 27–28.
109 Elizabeth Gilbert, *Big Magic: Creative Living Beyond Fear* (New York: Penguin Random House, 2015), 11–13, Google Books.

to keep your imagination private and build upon it between you and yourself. I need to believe in and accept my creative ideas. Author Steven Pressfield quotes W.H. Murray, saying, "Concerning all acts of initiative (and creation), there is one elementary truth, the ignorance of which kills countless ideas and splendid plans: that the moment one definitely commits oneself, then providence moves too."[110]

Trust is a big factor in intentionality. Once I trust my imagination, I expect more prudence. The idea that constructive imagination comes gradually from within creates more caution and credibility within the mind. I do not want to be proactive on a task based on wishful thinking as there is much more meaning and beauty in logical action.

Psychiatrist Carl Jung believed that we have active imagination. He defined this as how "the images have a life of their own and that the symbolic events develop according to their own logic—that is, of course, if your conscious reason does not interfere."[111]

This relates back to the balance aspect I place in proactivity. I need to take that step back to contemplate my subconscious thoughts and understand how I can prudently harness them in my conscious mind. These subconscious thoughts can initiate a new idea that I can be practical with for a lifetime. The symbolism from my subconscious mind can seem so

110 Steven Pressfield, *The War of Art: Break Through the Blocks and Win Your Inner Creative Battles* (New York: Rugged Land, 2002), 120.

111 Carl Jung, *Jung on Active Imagination* (New Jersey: Princeton University Press, 1997), 155–157, Google Books.

compelling and divine; it may make me feel so emotional that I will get a kick toward being proactive.

Jung says that since "by active imagination all the material is produced in a conscious state of mind, the material is far more rounded out than the dreams with their precarious language...the feeling-values are in it, and one can judge it by feeling."[112] Symbolism, if you completely understand it, creates meaning and feelings, and meaning and feelings create purpose. To convert the feelings to that organized regimen, I need to use critical thinking to decide which avenue I should take.

Like any of the other five principles in this book, imagination is an exercise. One innovative thought should lead to another. The difference between imagination and knowledge is that imagination is limitless. As Walt Disney once said: "Every child is born blessed with a vivid imagination. But just as a muscle grows flabby with disuse, so the bright imagination of a child pales in later years if he ceases to exercise it." My imagination may sound as crazy as the question, "What is the purpose of my identity?"

Moreover, I will never find out if I have any intentions of putting my ideas into action. The more willing I am to think innovatively, the more I train my brain to adapt to such a habit. On the other hand, if I daydream about past experiences and waste time making humor out of it, then I am losing an opportunity to think deeply about a lesson I can

---

112 Carl Jung, *Jung on Active Imagination* (New Jersey: Princeton University Press, 1997), 155–157, Google Books.

obtain from it. Every moment of our lives may not have a deep purpose, but I can reflect on words I have heard from past conversations and make twists to what their meanings were. This can motivate me to take further action on these personalized goals.

SYNCHRONICITY: THE MAGICAL MOMENTS

Carl Jung has a term for special coincidences: synchronicity. Jung describes this term thoroughly and accurately as something science cannot explain:

> Synchronicity designated the parallelism of time and meaning between psychic and psychophysical events, which scientific knowledge has thus far been unable to reduce to a common principle. The term explains nothing, it simply formulates the occurrence of meaningful coincidences which, in themselves, are chance happenings, but are so improbable that we must assume them to be based on some kind of principle, or on some property of the empirical world...from this it follows either that the psyche cannot be localized in space, or that space is relative to the psyche.[113]

I find the mystery of such meaningful events to be like the mystery of our subconscious. Still, I must be alert and be willing to listen to the messages my subconscious mind sends me. I just have to trust that my intentions will steer me in the right direction for a lucky series of synchronicities. This is

113 Kirby Surprise, *Synchronicity: The Art of Coincidence, Choice, and Unlocking Your Mind* (New Jersey: The Career Press, 2012), 35–37, Google Books.

not the same as serendipity because synchronicity is formed for us to think for ourselves through complexity. Meanwhile, serendipity gravitates more toward serving us with simple and sweet opportunities, as if we are given a gift with no action performed from our end.

These types of events do not purposely set themselves up in my favor; they are natural in their own way. It is how I perceive the events which makes the difference. Dr. Kirby Surprise summarizes this aspect, saying, "The events mirror our thoughts and concerns, giving the reflections added depth...(they) are like dreams that reveal bits of ourselves and leave us curious."[114] These events are like puzzle pieces that are doing the mental matching for me. My job is to use my imagination to understand their intentions and complete the puzzle through proactive action!

EMBRACE THE UNKNOWN
Imagination is unique since it is a product from the unknown. Our future ideas may stem from ideas known from the past, but we are potentially in the midst of the unknown. Will this idea work? Great ideas come and go; we may or may not obtain them entirely at a later time. The best technique to use is to write down the ideas as they come. These ideas come best when the mind is in a state of flow rather than being forced to think. With a notebook full of ideas, I am already set to build on ideas.

---

114 Kirby Surprise, *Synchronicity: The Art of Coincidence, Choice, and Unlocking Your Mind* (New Jersey: The Career Press, 2012), 56–57, Google Books.

On the other hand, if I am trying to think innovatively, then I am only creating resistance to my imagination. A mind with no expectations will invite an influx of ideas from unknown sources. A mind with expectations will expect magic to happen in the midst of stress and urgency for new ideas.

Imagination is vital for all success!

PART 3

THE SIX PRINCIPLES APPLIED IN *THE BRAIN HUT*

THE BRAIN HUT

* light bulb

The Thinking Room

* the ladder

The Misc. Room

The Chess Room

* the inner scepter

The Technology Room

The Silent Room

LIFE

The Social Life Room

* the mirror

—Nicholas B. D'Souza
December 2019

CHAPTER 1

THE BRAIN HUT

——

In Part Two, I explained why my six principles are important to intentionality and proactivity. I noted that they are important to exercise on a regular basis. Thinking is different from doing. Anyone can think about accomplishing great feats in life, but their habits tell the real story. The present is the future!

I am writing a book about my life every single day. Every year is a new chapter. I am twenty-four years old; therefore, I am in Chapter Twenty-Five. I cannot change the past chapters because they are already written. However, I can change my present to build a prosperous future.

In contemplating the primitive nature of my brain, I realized that my intentions and proactivity can help me push past my emotions and fears into a sophisticated world of knowledge, experiences, and accomplishments. In order to better explain the six principles in a modern-day context, I have created a map based on the mental "rooms" we enter in our everyday lives. I named it the Brain Hut because it is a simple, primitive map we can evaluate to adjust our intentions.

There are two main concepts about each of these rooms, the first being *what you do* and the second being *how much time you spend* in each of them. It begs the questions: "In regards to my intentions, how much time was I spending in this room, and what was I doing with that time?" *The golden rule of the Brain Hut is that you can only be in one room at a time.* So, let's get to the rooms' names!

The Brain Hut is made of five rooms. There are the four Time-out rooms: the Social Life Room, the Silent Room, the Technology Room, and one Miscellaneous Room. Then there is the Chess Room. Inside this hut framework, there is an invisible ladder which leads up to an invisible Thinking Room. Keep note that there is nothing inherently evil about any of these rooms.

The Brain Hut is a good way to measure time against our actions. When we move, we simply teleport from one room to the doorstep of another room. There is no relevance in the space between the rooms. I will provide a brief description of each of these rooms and explain how they relate to pro-activity and intentionality.

THE CHESS ROOM

The Chess Room is the golden room of the entire hut. This is where we execute our goals. Since the Brain Hut deals with intentionality, the Chess Room is where the proactive action takes place, while the Time-out rooms are where we casually spend our time away from our goals. This relates to my concept of balance in proactivity. All the rooms are action-based, but the Chess Room is different because it is goal-action-based.

Every chess game is not necessarily set up the same way. A competitive swimmer's swim season can include over one hundred fifty practices. One practice may have a series of hard workouts. Therefore, this chess game can be set as a full game with all thirty-two pieces on the board. On the other hand, another practice can be a short warm-up session just before a big Championship Meet. This may represent a chess match where all it takes is one piece to move once into a checkmate victory.

The whole purpose of the Brain Hut is to enter the Chess Room with prudence and to play with preparation and execution. The door is labeled "Life" because as long as we are living, our brains are functioning. Each effort will embellish one's "inner scepter." I make this reference due to the idea that we can all take the place of the "king" after we make an effort at something. Whether it is a failure or a successful match, we have gained experience and contemplative thought, which are successes in and of themselves.

Each failure may produce a common type of gem on the inner scepter. That gem represents a light of confidence, symbolizing persistence, which can help attain the end goal. A mediocre accomplishment, such as completing a homework assignment, will produce a valuable gem. On the other hand, an outstanding accomplishment, such as a nearly perfect SAT score, will produce a large, rare gem on the scepter.

These embellishments will not get destroyed as life moves on. They are symbols of past efforts and confidence to just keep trying. There is nothing to lose. In life, we want to embellish the inner scepter to its best quality. We may have a big, happy family with dozens having grandchildren in elderly age. However, there will not be a worse pain in life than the pain of regret in your future for not doing the things you wish you had in the past. I can get this perspective by how decorated my "inner scepter" is. As philosopher Thomas Carlyle once said, "No pressure, no diamonds."

In regards to success, your life is a symbol. The inner scepter's frame indicates the standards of your life's achievements.

Our opponent in the Chess Room is always the same one: Time. It would hurt to completely ignore the Chess Room and leave my inner scepter dormant and lacking iridescence. To enter the Chess Room is an accomplishment in and of itself. However, execution is the real matter. I can go into the Chess Room and get my laptop ready to work on a research paper. This can symbolize a full chess match in which I make the first pawn move. However, if I waste time spacing out, then Time has control over the game. I may lose my train of thought and not have a game plan to achieve my end goal: a concise, well-written paper. On the other hand, if I want to network with other people on LinkedIn for a specific project I am working on, then each outreach resembles a quick chess match: just one of my pieces and Time's king. All it takes is a simple message and "send" to put Time's king in checkmate.

This is how every chess game differs. Regardless of the style of the chess game, each game requires skill learned through experience. When I learn a new skill at work, I am developing it through Time. Time moves on as I perpetually train myself on a certain skill. Dr. Art Markman says, "The way that someone becomes an expert is to spend a lot of time learning about openings and endgames and strategies for playing the middle part of the game. Years of work give people specific knowledge about chess that they can use to play the game at the highest level."[115]

There is no greater joy for the inner scepter than to be proactive in the Chess Room for learning and experience. The Time-out rooms may give the scepter a spark to enter the Chess Room, but it is up to us to follow through.

In regards to the Time-out rooms, an action we may perceive to be related to the Technology Room, for example, may be related to the Chess Room instead. For instance, if I am playing video games for fun, then I am in the Technology Room since it is not goal-related. However, if I am working on a research paper on my laptop, then I am in the Chess Room since it is goal-related.

Life is hard. The harder we work in the Chess Room; the easier life will be. The more we ignore the Chess Room, the more difficult life will be. Time will never repay you the same amount that you waste throughout a lifetime. Having balance between the Chess Room and the Time-out rooms is important, but don't make the superfluous time spent in the Time-out rooms deprive you of a successful adventure in the golden room of the Hut!

---

115 Art Markman, *Smart Thinking: Three Essential Keys to Solve Problems, Innovate, and Get Things Done* (New York: Penguin Group, 2012), 18–20, Google Books.

THE THINKING ROOM'S RELATIONSHIP TO ALL THE ROOMS

We can easily have access to all the rooms, even the Chess Room. However, that does not mean that ninety percent of intentionality is just showing up. I can mentally walk into these rooms and merely just be present. This is where the Thinking Room plays a role. We are always thinking, whether our minds are wandering, or we are in contemplative thought. However, the Thinking Room pertains to constructive thinking. We can choose to climb the ladder to the Thinking Room or simply flow aimlessly.

The best question to ask in the Time-out rooms, in respect to the Thinking Room, is: "How can I use this current idea, in this moment, to execute in the Chess Room?" In the Chess Room, on the other hand, I can ask myself: "What is it about this chess game that I can learn from to take into my next series of chess games?"

The Thinking Room is always present, but it is up to me to be proactive in thinking for myself to properly prepare for execution. The best room that the Thinking Room can connect to is the Silent Room. Their connection produces a mental mirror that reveals the one person who can save you and produce your intentions. To harness the Thinking Room in any of the rooms is much better than to just simply be present and drift. It is not the end of the world to drift for temporary periods of time. After all, the rooms are named "Time-out" rooms for a reason. However, every single Hut room has a purposeful connection to the Thinking Room, so spark that light bulb!

TIME-OUT ROOM #1: THE TECHNOLOGY ROOM

I tend to spend a lot of time on my smartphone. Communication is great but the smartphone apps can steal my focus from my intentions. The Brain Hut focuses more on the caveats of the Technology Room than the benefits of it. Despite technology's advantages for connectivity with others, there is no better feeling than "to be," meaning to simply be present in the moment and away from our phones and other devices. The Technology Room is a room which should be approached with prudence. At times, it is better to entirely avoid it than to use it as an escape from a certain concern in any of the rooms. The best identity to have in this respect is to be a master of the Technology Room than to be a slave to it.

Social media can be a compelling source in the Technology Room, but the pertinent questions are: "How much time are you spending in it? How are you using it?" It is okay to enter the room to listen to music, but is the music time used superfluously to avoid a necessary task in the Chess Room? The Technology Room is a Hut room because our devices play a vital role in our daily lives for expedient use. Social media can be a good way to sugarcoat your problems with good posts. However, raw and genuine acts in the other rooms truly reveal one's character and personal ambitions.

TIME-OUT ROOM #2: THE SILENT ROOM

I need my "me" time on a regular basis. Silence is a great asset to harness that private conversation with ourselves, without any external distractions. Nobody else is walking in my shoes but me. Intentions are internal. Therefore, I must acknowledge this room as my personal mental space and base it throughout my daily life.

It is prudent to have doses of support from the Social Life Room and Technology Room, victories and failures in the Chess Room, and great ideas when connected to the Thinking Room. However, the Silent Room needs acknowledgment to bring all these experiences and ideas into perspective and add a prudent flavor to it. This room is a good way to build self-love and know one's self through a mirror that is created when we choose to be symbiotic with the Thinking Room. No external factor can destroy this mirror. It is a real and raw reflection of our flaws and beauty. The mirror is the greatest gift to make the proper adjustments to how we approach the other Time-out rooms and the Chess Room.

On the other hand, running away to this room for isolation only creates a sense of insecurity and a lack of attention to the Thinking Room. No mirror is present, only a reflection of bad experiences from the other rooms. We have a decision to look at the silence aspect as either a glass half full or half empty. We want to block the world out in the Silent Room to think for ourselves rather than as a source of escape.

TIME-OUT ROOM #3: THE SOCIAL LIFE ROOM

Relationships are everything. We need them. The Social Life Room is a face-to-face environment. Social communication on technology is restricted to the Technology Room. The more we enter the Social Life Room and search for trust, the more chances we have to gain new friends for a lifetime. Relationships contribute to perspective and other people's purposes. In a way, we can feel motivated to chase after our purpose after understanding the "why" behind other people's intentions.

There are people who we find authentic help from, people who we find an unhealthy comfort around, and people who share a negative attitude with us. Usually, the positive people make this room a good space for optimism and support toward our goals in the Chess Room. On the other hand, the bad aspect stems from the negative people who may delude who we are through ignorant and arrogant speech. The critics can plant "bad seeds" or delusions into our heads to disrupt our focus. It is up to us to be proactive toward confronting such people and to immediately remove these bad seeds from the Chess Room.

In the conversations you have with others in this room, it is best to focus on ideas over events or other people. Ideas can pull together two minds into one constructive idea. Why bother deeply discussing celebrities' lives when these celebrities do not even know about your existence? If I can't walk into a Starbucks and get my coffee without being asked what my name is, then I sure have a lot of work to do to be recognized for leaving a significant mark on the world.

TIME-OUT ROOM #4: THE MISCELLANEOUS ROOM

The Miscellaneous Room can be whatever you like, and there can be a countless number of them. One example can be the "pleasure reading" room. It is not necessarily an action toward an end goal, but just a good time-out to take a break from the Chess Room. Just like any other Time-out room, the Miscellaneous Room can spark an idea to organize into a goal-related action. When connected with the Thinking Room, I need to trust the process and be willing to accept any intention that unexpectedly comes to my mind for a greater purpose.

HOW THE BRAIN HUT MAP WORKS

The Brain Hut map can be viewed in two different ways: one to meditate on throughout the day, and one to write down on paper at the end of the day.

MEDITATION

For the meditation aspect, you have to mentally focus on the Brain Hut map and reflect on how you will "squeeze the orange" (getting the best quality out of a task) in the current room you are in to maximize your results. For example, when you are in the Chess Room, you have to acknowledge the fact that you are in the midst of an opportunity to change your life for the better. So how are you going to handle that room in regards to what you are doing to change your life? When you are in the Technology Room, are you on your phone to simply catch up with your news feed and move on to something meaningful? Or is social media a constant escape to view the same content meaninglessly over and over again?

It is easy to write down on paper what you want to do at the beginning of each day. However, just checking each activity off on paper does not mean that you performed the task efficiently. This is why it is necessary to plan your day's schedule outside of a Brain Hut map and harness the Brain Hut map mentally during the day's activities. You want to envision what your Brain Hut map will look like at the end of the day, knowing you gave maximized effort!

PAPER

This leads to the paper aspect. When drawing your own Brain Hut map at the end of the day, you need to set a specific time frame. An ideal time frame is the twenty-four-hour day, but it can vary. You can have two different Brain Huts showing your habits in one year on one hut and your habits in the next year in another hut. You can even make a Brain Hut of your activities within a five-hour time frame. You can make as many Miscellaneous Rooms as possible, referring to whatever activities are outside the scope of technology, your social life, your private life, and your goals.

The point of this end of the day activity is to be cognizant of the activities you have done in each of the rooms and how long you spent in them. For example, you can branch out from the Technology Room and note that you spent twenty percent of the day playing video games. Does this contribute well to your goals in the Chess Room? This can point out any flaws that must be brought to your attention that show why your inner scepter is not as embellished as you expect it to be.

* * *

To encapsulate all of this, there are two important questions to ask yourself in your Hut:

1. Was the Thinking Room relevant to my time here?

2. How does this relate to the Chess Room and my inner scepter?

Your choice of activity and how you spent your time in each room is a good illustration of your intentions from that specific day. Again, thinking is different from action. Do your actions correlate with your intentions?

* * *

For the rest of Part Three, I will group the six principles in groups of three- sets of pairs in each. I explained in Part Two why they are important to proactivity, but I will explain them in the context of silence, social environment, and technology. In drawing our map, we can understand where our status is at the end of the day. How much time did we dedicate to the Chess Room? The smallest victories are the ones which add up. An athlete taking a day off to stretch is a Chess Room activity in and of itself since it is a cause for the greater good.

After sharing the six principles within these rooms' contexts, I will share personal stories, primary interview stories, and secondary stories from some of the world's successful people on what their Brain Huts look like. We all have this rigid Brain Hut map to refer to, but what separates the best from the mediocre are the intentions and proactive actions from one activity to the next.

CHAPTER 2

HABITS AND TIME MANAGEMENT

Habits and time management are two principles which need to be correlated in order to produce an efficient approach to one's intentions. I included single-tasking in the time management chapter in Part Two because it describes the quality aspect of time management. Just because I have the right quantity of time management for a certain task does not mean I am actually carrying out my intentions.

CHESS, SILENT, AND MISCELLANEOUS ROOMS

We can get carried away with the "thrill of victory." However, how do we define victory?

The Chess Room is for serious goals which can inspire others, elevate our character and reputation, and leave a significant mark on the world. There is a thrill when the king stands tall at the end of the chess match. However, this thrill should not be comparable to an insignificant achievement.

For example, if I have a habit of playing recreational basketball to break a sweat and exercise, then I should not feel that my inner scepter is embellished every time I win a game. Maybe my strategies and focus are good to exercise the Thinking Room, but I must not fool myself into thinking I am in the Chess Room. Instead, I am in the Miscellaneous Room.

To fully understand this, I must be cognizant of the successful thrills I experience on a daily basis in the Silent Room. I have to shut the world out and think of what activities I am doing in each of the Brain Hut rooms, and if any of them are hindering me, quality- or time-wise. Our endeavors should be meaningful and sustainable if they are to be placed in the Chess Room. This does not mean the victories we experience in the Time-out rooms are unnecessary, though. The question we must ask is whether we are confusing them with chess victories or not. The Chess Room is where we should primarily place our habits and time!

THE HABIT OF ENTERING THE TECHNOLOGY ROOM (HABITS)

To start this section, it is important to understand the bad habit of using the smartphone. Smartphone apps have limitless information, and it is easy to access them with a click of a button. While this is useful, it is dangerous to overuse the phone since it can waste our time in the other rooms and become an uncontrollable habit that is hard to resist. Unless there is a constructive way to use the phone to communicate with others, I usually try to stay away from the phone to avoid superfluous time in the Technology Room. Instead, I can be present in a different room, away from the virtual world.

Practicality in reality—especially in the Chess Room—can help me get in a rhythm to do something great for my inner scepter.

Chartered psychologist Daria J. Kuss, from Nottingham Trent University, says, "From the perspective of neural circuity, excessive and prolonged engagement with the Internet may lead to changes in the structure of the brain...excessive and prolonged engagement may lead to desensitization to the pleasurable effects of Internet usage over time, requiring higher doses (i.e., increased amounts of time investment) to result in similar benefits."[116]

In Part Two, I discussed that our brains have high activity at the start of every new habit. When I download a new app or start a new video game, I have different ideas regarding what the virtual world can lead me. Once I engage more and more, I learn new things and want to delve deeper into the pleasures of the Technology Room, but this has no relevance to my goals in the Chess Room.

Rather than be proactive by making and setting my own goals, I find ways to meet the goals of the video games or express myself on social media to others. There is nothing wrong with self-expression, but I need to avoid the habit of caring about what other people think of me on a technology platform. Other people are not going to do the work for me. A good habit in the Chess Room starts with a good fear regarding the struggle of what is yet to come in the process. A

---

116 Daria J. Kuss and Mark D. Griffiths, *Internet Addiction in Psychotherapy* (England: Palgrave Macmillan, 2015), 12–13, Google Books.

bad habit in the Technology Room, on the other hand, starts with wonder, and then a superfluous time consumption of the pleasurable aspects of the virtual world.

Cal Newport quotes English writer Arnold Bennett in relation to expedient pleasures, which consume too much time. Bennett says, "Put more thought into your leisure time. In other words, this strategy suggests that when it comes to your relaxation, don't default to whatever catches your attention at the moment, but instead dedicate some advance thinking to the question of how you want to spend your 'day within a day.'"[117]

Since the Technology Room is a Time-out room, it is unhealthy to develop a bad habit of diving into the virtual world for self-satisfaction, especially with no connection to the Thinking Room. If I establish a rhythm with the Thinking Room in any Time-out room, I will find it less appealing to waste time in the Technology Room. This is because I will feel I am working toward something valuable as opposed to succumbing to instant gratification.

The best solution I implement to avoid excessive time in the Technology Room is simply staying away from it. This is another habit in and of itself because the initial stage will feel weird. If I lock my phone in a drawer in a different room than mine, then it may feel like it does not exist in my head. I will feel no need to reach for it or ponder on the numerous posts I can gain information from.

---

117 Cal Newport, *Deep Work: Rules for Focused Success in a Distracted World* (New York: Hachette Book Group, 2016), 177–179, Google Books.

The "dings" we hear on the phone can cause a rush of excitement because someone took the time to send a message to us. This lust for virtual communication is a bad habit, as we are not single-tasking. Our minds shift from the Technology Room to the Chess Room. It is usually not guaranteed that we know the intentions of the text sender—even if they express their "emotions" through certain emojis—so it is best to not waste time pondering their mindset in the Technology Room, but rather focus on the goals in front of us on the chessboard!

CHESS ROOM AND TECHNOLOGY ROOM (SINGLE-TASKING)

When we are executing our goals, it is important to get into a mindset of harnessing the Thinking Room and implementing good ideas while in practice. Social media tends to distract us and instill a fear of missing out on new information. In regards to fragmented attention, Cal Newport says that social media apps "offer personalized information arriving on an unpredictable intermittent schedule—making them massively addictive and therefore capable of severely damaging your attempts to schedule and succeed with any act of concentration."[118]

When I yearn to achieve a goal in the Chess Room, I cannot alternate into a different room sporadically. This is not single-tasking, and it will divert my focus every time I come back to the Chess Room. For example, if I am working on an assignment in the Chess Room but reach for my phone

---

118 Cal Newport, *Deep Work: Rules for Focused Success in a Distracted World* (New York: Hachette Book Group, 2016), 170–172, Google Books.

every fifteen minutes, I will have to remember which "move" to do when I get back into the Chess Room. In other words, I will have lost my train of thought.

In regards to the fear of missing out—or FOMO—Newport says, "...part of what makes social media insidious is that the companies that profit from your attention have succeeded with a masterful marketing coup: convincing our culture that if you don't use their products you might miss out."[119]

At the end of the day, not much of what I read online pertains to my goals. My intentions stem internally. Therefore, I am the master of my own craft. It is definitely fine to gain knowledge of current events and issues. However, in the midst of work in the Chess Room, nothing else should matter but the task at hand. The external information of the world can wait to be read later.

This is where time management comes in. If I set a time for social media news and stick to it, I will have no desire to alternate back and forth just to receive new information as soon as I can. It will always be there. This is a struggle because, as human beings, we crave new information. Professor Adam Gazzaley says, "...at our core we are information-seeking creatures, so behaviors that maximize information accumulation are optimal, at least from that viewpoint. This notion is supported by findings that molecular and physiological mechanisms that originally developed in our brain

_____

119 Ibid. 172–175.

to support food foraging for survival have now evolved in primates to include information foraging."[120]

With this is mind, we have a simple solution when struggling in the middle of our chess matches: stay out of the Technology Room. It is best to work with what is in front of us rather than digest too much information, some of which may be unnecessary or fake, such as on social media.

SILENT ROOM AND TECHNOLOGY ROOM (SINGLE-TASKING)

I view the Silent Room as a vital room to give undivided attention to. It should be a good habit to always visit and harness the Thinking Room to think about one's day with no external distractions. I may get in the habit of pulling my phone from my pocket to check the latest social media updates. However, this does not keep me present in the moment.

I am not necessarily referring to meditation in the Silent Room, but the simple act of existing with a subtle reflection of one's day or past experiences. I believe this is a good practice to recollect how I feel in the moment and if there are any insecurities which linger in my mind. I must face these insecurities I see in my mental mirror. The most important conversation I can have is with myself.

The Technology Room may be an escape from my reality, or I may run to the Social Life Room to escape my isolation. I

---

120 Larry D. Rosen and Adam Gazzaley, *The Distracted Mind: Ancient Brains in a High-Tech World* (Massachusetts: The MIT Press, 2016), 29–31, Google Books.

create my own intentions and proactive choices. Therefore, I need to develop a habit of making memories and a relationship with myself. I have to use time management to decide which time frame of the day I will dedicate to "me" time.

CHESS, SILENT, AND SOCIAL LIFE ROOMS (SNEAKERS MENTALITY)

Sometimes in the Chess Room, we may be confronted by "bad seeds" near the front door. We create these bad seeds if we accept other people's negative commentary in the Social Life Room. The more we digest it and let it sink in, the more these bad seeds grow.

A good, proactive approach is the *sneakers mentality*. When you look at your sneakers, you only think of yourself because you are their owner. Therefore, nobody has any right to judge your actions because they do not know the background of your mentality within your sneakers' journey.

We want to take some time to channel this mentality in the Silent Room and establish a habit out of it. To do this, we must completely block out any past or expected negative commentary from the Social Life Room and remind ourselves: "I will execute my moves in the Chess Room regardless of anything that comes my way because only I can be the best judge of myself." This will keep your single-tasking skills focused and, therefore, make your time spent in the Chess Room efficient. Talk is cheap. The points on the chessboard are all that matter at the end of the day.

SOCIAL LIFE ROOM (HABITS)

My social circle is a vital factor in my habits. I have to be cognizant of the people I spend time with in the Social Life Room because they are the people I share with and receive ideas from. Nobody else is going to make my goals for me. I need to know what goals I can be practical about and then find the right people with similar goals or good character in respect to their own respective goals. I can learn from others' integrity without taking it over the limit and emulating them.

Author Stephen R. Covey says, "As we become independent-proactive, centered in our principles, value driven, and able to organize and execute around the priorities in our life with integrity—we then can choose to become interdependent—capable of building rich, enduring, highly productive relationships with other people."[121]

I can only understand the internal struggle it takes to reach my goals. However, a mutual understanding of one another's paths in the Social Life Room can give me a good boost, allowing me to think: "We are in this together. I know I can find a way to contribute to someone else's journey."

Author Napoleon Hill has a concept known as the "Master Mind." He defines this as the "coordination of knowledge and effort, in a spirit of harmony, between two or more people, for the attainment of a definite purpose."[122] The Chess Room journey can be lonely. After all, nobody else is making my

---

121 Stephen R. Covey, *The 7 Habits of Highly Effective People* (Miami: FranklinCovey Co., 2015), 233–235, Google Books.
122 Napoleon Hill, *Think and Grow Rich* (think-and-grow-rich-ebook.com, 2007), 168.

moves for me. However, there is a strong sense of motivation when I am linked with other people's intentions in the Chess Room. As Hill states, there is harmony in the Master Mind. For example, as an author, I may sometimes have deluded thoughts about my imagination and feel that my work is not noteworthy. However, in the midst of doing my writing with a fellow author, there is a "third mind" present which helps me transcend beyond all my delusions. This energy propels me forward with confidence, knowing that there is another person who is working on their craft in their own respective way. It gives a diverse atmosphere and makes me more cognizant of the specific role I play in comparison to the roles other people play.

Loneliness may cause chaos and a loss of direction. It is conducive to develop a habit to revisit my friends—who harness the Thinking Room as efficiently as I do—at least twice a week. Together, in our own ways, we become a strong force which cannot be broken. After our chess games are played, win or lose, we can all reconvene and celebrate each other's progress. I look at my ambitious friends and I as toothpicks. I can easily feel broken if I neglect to learn and contribute to others. However, in the "Master Mind," I am wrapped with my fellow toothpicks, or friends, by a rubber band. Nothing can break any of us in this tight bond.

The best time management skill in the Social Life Room is to set time for driven friends, but also to avoid as much time possible with the folly folks. If I do not see potential in cooperation, and only see ignorance, then it is best to ignore wasting time with the people who choose to be aimless and ignorant of the Chess Room.

It is important to understand a meaningful bond with others in the Social Life Room. Empty laughter is a caveat to bonding because it produces a "good feeling." However, there is no substance to it and no relevance to the Chess Room. This does not mean that it is detrimental to enjoy nonsensical laughter with others. However, it is important to not make it a habit, and to set it aside on occasion. Because the Thinking Room is not involved in empty laughter, if developed into a bad habit, it can be an ideal escape from the Chess Room's reality. Empty laughter is different from normal laughter. Normal laughter has a constructive build into the laugh based on a logical premise mixed with humor. Empty laughter is originated on the idea that at least two people should make up illogical and foolish humor just for the sake of attaining the expedient end: laughter. For example, if two people feel superior in sharing negative criticism about someone else, then they can make an ignorant statement and immediately delve into empty laughter. On the other hand, if someone thinks outside the box about a certain scenario and draws in humor, then the laugher is normal.

As you build on a habit, there must be a passion toward what you want. It is the ideal way to be sustainable in the process. The worst idea to have is that there is a magical formula in the Social Life Room. Perhaps there is something you see someone else do—such as drink a specific sports drink— which makes you think that it is the trick to a more successful Chess Room match? This thinking is unnecessary. We must approach the Social Life Room as if everything we hear and see from others is not one hundred percent legitimate. There may be a good deal of conversation someone has just to sugarcoat their reality. We must balance the habit of being alert to some intriguing conversations, which may be useful for analysis in the Thinking Room for a later time, whilst processing all external information prudently.

It is very important to be proactive in thinking about our friends who know how to talk for hours upon entering the Social Life Room. Time management is key for balance in the Chess Room. As long as we set boundaries for when a conversation may end, with the respectful choice of words, we can adjust from the Social Life Room to the Chess Room in a timely manner.

SOCIAL LIFE ROOM (TECH AND SINGLE-TASKING)

Any hard task in the Chess Room requires integrity and rigid focus. The Technology Room provides an expedient mentality for communication. If we can take a time-out from the Technology Room and focus on our human attributes in our face-to-face conversations in the Social Life Room, then we can have very powerful and meaningful memories of our relationships. At the end of the day, the smartphone provides messages in the form of bubbles. Real-life conversation provides an authentic voice that is distinct from each human being. I can get so carried away with the instant use of communication on my phone that I completely forget this realization.

Researcher Sherry Turkle says, "At first, we speak through machines and forget how essential face-to-face conversation is to our relationships, our creativity, and our capacity for empathy. At a second, we take a further step and speak not just through machines but to machines."[123]

It is proof at a dining table where I see everyone on their phones instead of being present in face-to-face conversation. The Social Life Room is built on face-to-face conversations. The Technology Room is based on virtual conversation. In the dining room reference, every person on their phone is in the Technology Room despite being physically right next to each other. When I think of having dinner at the dining table, I think of the people I will eat with and the conversations we may have—this is my time management focus. These conversations may never come to fruition if I decide to exit the Social Life Room and spend superfluous time in the Technology Room while eating.

The sad part is that I do not even realize it goes against my time management while I am doing it! If I build on this bad habit, then I can miss out on potential ideas and meaningful conversations with others. After all, the Chess Room is built on ideas and meaning. They are real and not virtual.

HABITS AND TIME MANAGEMENT BRAIN HUT RECAP

It is important to make a schedule and use time management to organize our time in the Chess Room and work toward our goals, to dedicate quality time for ambitious friends on a great journey, to build a habit of having personal conversations with ourselves, and to get into the habit of avoiding

---

123 Sherry Turkle, *Reclaiming Conversation: The Power of Talk in a Digital Age* (Penguin Books, 2015), 12–13, Google Books.

the Technology Room unless it's for an urgent communication purpose, or if we set a reasonable time frame for social media updates.

In regard to Chess Room progress, the greatest feats take trial and error. Time management should be dedicated to habits. It is easy to go all in one day on a hard task, but consistency is important. How will time management with a new group of friends in the Social Life Room affect your habits in a different room, such as the Silent Room? Perhaps you need to adjust time frames to give the proper respect to both your ambitious friends and your own "me" time.

We can hesitate at times about whether we want to enter the Chess Room because of the intimidation of establishing a new habit. Life is short and it is a risk, so we might as well put in the time in the Chess Room rather than find comfort in the Time-out rooms. Time waits for nobody!

Since life is a symbol, we need stability. The Chess Room is a great source to be practical on constructive habits. As we obtain more king victories, we learn more about ourselves. It's all about being proactive in maintaining our habits and time management. The Thinking Room will obtain more ideas based on past experiences as we continue to mentally grow throughout our lives.

Brain Hut Acronym for Single-Tasking and Multitasking

Strategic (The Chess Room requires undivided attention when executing a step-by-step process.)

Internal (Our internal thoughts from the Thinking Room can overcome the internal and external distractions and interruptions from any of the other rooms.)

Nonchalant (Fixate on the moment in calmness and do not switch gears irrationally.)

Gems (Through failures and successes, the inner scepter will be embellished by our undivided attention and efforts.)

Love (How much love do we have for the chess game? Are we fully locked in?)

Encapsulate (The number and quality of our chess games are encapsulated by the sum of our time spent focused on our goal.)

Malevolence (Fragmented attention will only lead to frustration with ourselves along a success path.)

Unstoppable (A bad habit of multitasking may spin someone in circles around the Brain Hut.)

Lazy (A rigorous task may be too much, so someone may procrastinate in another room for a long time and only occasionally return to the Chess Room within a certain time frame.)

Teleporting (The mind is not focused on one specific activity in one room—instead, it flip-flops here and there.)

Idleness (A true goal means something so special that someone would die for it and go all in with a minimum of one hundred percent. Half-hearted effort equates to zero percent effort.)

CHAPTER 3

SELF-CARE AND SELF-CONTROL

In Part Two, I discussed sleep, healthy eating, and exercise as good habits for self-care. They make us function properly to get the best out of the Thinking Room and execute efficiently in the Chess Room. In regards to self-control, I discussed the importance of delaying instant gratification for the sake of one's goals. When the grind gets tough, it is easy to simply leave the Chess Room and find comfort in a different room. I paired these principles because both require self-discipline and a step out of the comfort zone.

In order to exercise self-control, it is essential to exercise self-care by eating right, getting optimal hours of sleep, and regularly exercising throughout the week. Self-control and self-care are both proactive elements to use against the reactive temptations of pleasure. Do more of what is right, and life will be easier. Do more of what is pleasurable, and life will get harder.

TECHNOLOGY ROOM AND CHESS ROOM (SELF-CONTROL)

Sometimes when doing what is right means doing what is hard, I can find comfort in the Technology Room. Social media is an ideal place to find that comfort through the "love" we receive from our social media friends. Dr. Pavica Sheldon says, "One of the rewarding experiences that might result in an increase in dopamine is the use of social media to play games, receive "likes" and "favorites" on Instagram photos.... In fact, when someone likes your Instagram post, it is a very similar experience to taking a drug as far as your brain is concerned."[124]

Since the long and challenging chess games of our life require a step-by-step process, it is easy to get that "end of the game victory feeling" by just moving to the Technology Room and making a post for "likes." Emojis and "good to read" messages give us that instant pleasure. The Chess Room usually requires a rigorous and thorough mindset in connection with the Thinking Room. There is nothing evil about social media, per se; however, the question is if we are using it as an escape.

People may view my post in different perspectives and give me that "like." This is why I view such pleasures as superficial. I see a list of "likes" and feel like a well-liked person. However, some may like my post just for the sake of "liking" it, and others because they actually do like it. The comfortable escape to the Technology Room makes what is superficial

---

124 Pavica Sheldon, Philipp A. Rauschnabel, and James M. Honeycutt, *The Dark Side of Social Media: Psychological, Managerial, and Societal Perspectives* (UK: Elsevier, 2019), 26–27, Google Books.

feel important and my important duties feel superficial. The best solution is to shut off the phone and place it across from you whilst in the Chess Room.

The Technology Room is important for communication, but there is one thing which is not fully present: body language. We have to be present within the Thinking Room and envision ourselves talking to someone in the Technology Room the same way we do in the Social Life Room. If we do not, there is a dysfunctional aspect present in the Technology Room, which results in objectifying the other person. We cannot settle for this mentality because it feels expedient and comfortable to get what we want out of a conversation. There must be acknowledgement that the other person is a human being, and thus we must have a sense of empathy.

TECHNOLOGY ROOM (SELF-CONTROL) AND SELF-CARE ROOM (SLEEP AND NUTRITION)

NUTRITION

In Part Two, I discussed how pleasure can be relative. If I am in the Technology Room watching entertaining shows on television, I am absorbing pleasure. Entertainment has no relevance to my personal goals. Now, let's say there is a box of sugar cookies on the table in front of me. Since I am in a pleasurable state of mind, I can crave for more pleasure in consuming one cookie after another, despite not feeling hungry. In the midst of it all, I do not feel anything bad. Moving from one pleasure to another feels normal since I have already initiated a comfort status in watching TV.

However, at the end of the day when I view my Brain Hut map and acknowledge my lack of self-control—bouncing from the Technology Room to the Miscellaneous Room which, in this case, is the room where I focus on eating—I may understand why I feel unmotivated the next day to enter the Chess Room. Psychotherapist Julie M. Simon says, "When we regularly eat in the absence of physical hunger cues, choose unhealthy comfort foods, or eat when we are already full, something is out of balance somewhere…missing or have poorly developed self-regulation skills—especially the ability to connect to, or attune to and be mindful of, their internal world, and to regulate their feelings, moods, impulses, and behaviors."[125] Utilize the Thinking Room and prevent yourself from indulging in eating for pleasure in order to continue the momentum from the pleasures of technology. This can lead to an unhealthy habit!

SLEEP

I have an interesting point that the same concept explained above applies to sleep. When I am in bed, I am in a comfortable setting. If I have a habit of scrolling through my social media feed at the end of the day, then I can transfer to the Technology Room to add more to my comfort. I may think that the day is ended, and I have no purpose to be in the Chess Room until tomorrow. However, there is a caveat to wasting time on the phone that is meant for sleeping. Research has shown that "the use of…devices…before bedtime prolongs the time it takes to fall asleep, delays the circadian clock,

---

125 Julie M. Simon, *When Food is Comfort: Nurture Yourself Mindfully, Rewire Your Brain, and End Emotional Eating* (California: New World Library, 2018), 40–41, Google Books.

suppresses levels of the sleep-promoting hormone melatonin, reduces the amount and delays the timing of REM sleep, and reduces alertness the following morning."[126]

The effects of the phone are credited to its short-wavelength-enriched light, or artificial light exposure. The best solution is to set the phone across the Self-care (or Sleeping) Room from my bed. If I have an alarm clock, then I can place my phone literally in a different room in my house. The whole idea is to not have any intention to touch it, even in the middle of the night. The poor habit of seeking pleasure, through the device, will have us wake up unmotivated to act upon our intentions in the Chess Room. Instead of spending time on the phone while in bed, how about using the Thinking Room to reflect on the day? Did you enter the Chess Room today? How much did you accomplish? How can you get better tomorrow?

SOCIAL LIFE ROOM (SELF-CONTROL)

CLOSE FRIENDS AND WEAK TIES

Relationships with family and friends are very important. We cannot pretend that we do not need them. However, we must be cognizant of how they vary. When I feel disappointed or bogged down by my Chess Room failures, I need to have self-control and harness the Thinking Room to create the next steps. A tempting pleasure may be to enter the Social Life Room and spend time with my "comfort" friends. This

---

126 "Evening use of light-emitting eReaders negatively affects sleep, circadian timing, and next-morning alertness," PNAS, accessed October 9, 2020.

type of friend tells me things that I want to hear, such as, "It is okay. You tried your best. Let's celebrate your efforts." While this may be encouraging in some way, I need friends who will have a serious conversation with me, discussing the source of my failures and how I can be proactive about it. Instead, I am "using" my comfort friends for consolation rather than having a raw conversation with them.

Other than soft compliments, another aspect of comfort friends is they do not have a well-established inner scepter. If I want to improve my own inner scepter, it is unhealthy to seek comfort by surrounding myself with friends who do not measure up to my ambitions and success. The solution to this social comfort trap is to find the friends who will stop me when I am ready to throw in the towel.

In regards to our best friends, it may hurt to see the aggressive side of motivation from someone we value and hold close. If not handled properly, it can create tension within the relationship. Therefore, it is important to always develop "weak ties" in the Social Life Room—relationships with people who you are not necessarily close with but have a strong, confidential relationship with in regards to a certain goal. There is more freedom in these relationships to move toward your personal intentions. If there is an instance of tension, then there is not much to be concerned about because the weak tie is nothing more than an acquaintance. This does not mean that we should let go of our close friends who do not have the same mentalities with us regarding our goals. Instead, we should keep our goals private from them and focus on why we like them to keep the relationship sustainable.

DEAL WITH THE STRUGGLE OF BEING YOU!

The Social Life Room can be filled with people who "go with the wind." These people will gravitate toward the "noise," or compelling body language. If someone receives a positive vibe from someone's actions, the recipient may want to emulate that person's behavior. This may provide some comfort and even motivation for short-term enthusiasm. However, it is important to not let the Social Life Room determine our sense of identity. The Silent Room is where we must come to terms with who we really are, no matter how uncomfortable we may feel with our character and reputation.

We all have a deep purpose on this planet. Celebrities—such as actors, athletes, and political figures—can serve as idols to us. However, we should not have deep conversations in the Social Life Room about our idols' personal lives on a consistent basis. We must ask ourselves: "Are these celebrities discussing amongst themselves about our personal lives and goals?" No! They do not even know we exist. The sun and moon shine in their own time. To attract the right people, we must know how our worth differs from others and not make comparisons.

There needs to be a sense of pride in our uniqueness among others in the Social Life Room. We cannot change for anybody else. Just as a cat does not chase a human being for attention, we must focus on ourselves and not chase others in the Social Life Room. A cat, in general, will gravitate toward something which will attract it. For example, food. In a way, we must make someone else in the Social Life Room in the position of this cat attracted to our success as a source of inspiration. If we build our successful security—such as our character—we can attract the cat.

THE CUP

It is important to harness the Thinking Room in the Social Life Room and be cognizant of how others may perceive our character. The worst hit to take is a false reputation that others ascribe to us. If we want to spread our Chess Room success in the Social Life Room, we must have a "cup" to fill and pour to others. For every gem we add to our inner scepter, we have a dose of water added in the cup! There are others who may cause you pain, whether it's a heartbreak or rejection, but it is up to you to either convert this poison into healthy water in your cup, or let it drain your current fill.

SOCIAL LIFE ROOM AND SELF-CARE ROOM (NUTRITION AND EXERCISE)

One of the best solutions to overcoming bad eating habits and getting motivated to exercise is to find the right people in the Social Life Room who will keep you grounded and focused on what is right. In regards to nutrition, if I have a habit of eating fast food every Friday night, then it would be helpful to associate myself with someone who is on a strict diet. This will make me feel guilty when entering the Self-care Room with someone who has better health standards than I have.

Sometimes I may lose drive in going to the gym and working out by myself. A workout buddy can improve my exercise routine in the Self-care Room. Valerie Latona, CEO of VL Health Media, says, "Research has shown that a partner's better fitness habits can rub off on us, inspiring us to reach higher levels of conditioning…these researchers found that having a more fit buddy could increase your workout time and intensity by as much as two hundred percent."[127] A mutual presence in the Self-care Room can sure scrub off any desires for quitting and seeking comfort.

SILENT ROOM (SELF-CARE AND SELF-CONTROL)

Sometimes it is hard to maintain self-control in the Silent Room. There may be an urge for noise and action elsewhere. Chinese philosopher Lao Tzu once said, "If you are depressed, you are living in the past. If you are anxious, you are living in the future. If you are at peace, you are living in the present." Why not take this time of boredom to find that peace? Along with that, why not also train the mind to handle resistance against any external distractions?

Cal Newport says, "...to succeed with deep work you must rewire your brain to be comfortable resisting distracting stimuli. This doesn't mean that you have to eliminate distracting behavior; it's sufficient that you instead eliminate the ability of such behaviors to hijack your attention."[128] These temptations may include unnecessary sleep, unhealthy food, comfort friends, or virtual entertainment.

ARE WE INHALING OR EXHALING?

If we are "inhaling," we are absorbing knowledge and working on building ourselves in the Chess Room. If we are "exhaling," we are looking for stress relief and downtime in

---

127 Valerie Latona, "The Big Benefits of Exercise Buddies," AARP, accessed October 9, 2020.

128 Cal Newport, *Deep Work: Rules for Focused Success in a Distracted World* (New York: Hachette Book Group, 2016), 137–139, Google Books.

the Time-out rooms. In the Silent Room, it is important to ask ourselves how much time we spend inhaling or exhaling. When we feel that we are inhaling, we may actually be exhaling.

THE SILENT ROOM IS THE ULTIMATE TIME-OUT ROOM
Every time we enter the Silent Room, we need to feel confident in the person reflected in the mirror. There is only one person who you spend your whole life with, and that is you! If you have a problem with that, there is a serious issue. How can we build that confidence? Self-care. You want to see a healthy body committed to a positive sleep, exercise, and nutrition routine.

The Silent Room can possess a crucial reset button to harness in the other rooms. In order to avoid any detrimental comfort, we need to take advantage of the room's silence and block out all external noise and distractions. In doing this, we blind ourselves to any negativity in the near future.

Happiness is found within. Only we can control our happiness; nothing external can do so. Extroverts may receive energy from others to do their actions, but the energy is not doing the action, per se. Therefore, it is important to develop a good mood in the Silent Room to emit into any other room. Good vibes create a good perspective, and a bad mood may create a delusional and negative perspective on the same matter. Everything is internal!

* * *

Regardless of how constructive these choices are, there should be some time set aside to bond with the Thinking Room in the Silent Room for that mirror. It will bring out the hard questions in you, which will stabilize your self-control. As badly as I want to run away to comfort, I know I have to go through my insecurities to be proactive! The Silent Room is where you feel closest to the real answers.

THE THINKING ROOM (SELF-CONTROL)

Regardless of which room you are in, there are two mentalities to attach to the Thinking Room: the "divine vs. secular" mentality, and the "sustainable" mentality.

DIVINE VS. SECULAR MENTALITY ("1" VS. "2")

When you think "divine," you usually think of heaven and a perpetual presence. When you think "secular," you think of the temporary pleasures of the world. Let's make "1" resemble divine and "2" resemble secular. When you seek 1, you are seeking a high mentality and grit. Along with 1, you sustain the 1 and naturally obtain more of 2. However, if you seek 2, then you will eventually lose both 1 and 2. Money is a good example for 2. Money does not grow on trees. You can desperately work several dead end jobs just for the sake of money, but also lose much "me" time in the Silent room to meditate on 1 (a sustainable and single focused job career). When you focus on 1, you can have the good comfort of knowing you are climbing the ladder and have records of promotions for future employers.

For another example, healthy foods can be 1 and sugary foods can be 2. The more healthy foods you consume, the more tolerance you can have for a few sugary foods throughout the week. However, the more sugary foods you have, the more unhealthy pleasure you obtain and the fewer healthy eating habits your body is familiar with. Your body is adapting to pleasure foods that it does not understand right from wrong with the proper nutrients the body needs.

SUSTAINABILITY MENTALITY

After a big victory in the Chess Room or a great time with friends in the Social Life Room, we may ride off what we feel is a "high"–that intense feeling of joy which lingers after a great accomplishment or social event.

But what is inevitable? That the high will eventually die down.

Once the high dies down, we may feel a bit sad. Therefore, we can search for comfort to compensate for this empty feeling. The best proactive approach is to connect the Thinking Room with the Silent Room and gather our thoughts as to why we feel a certain "high." It is okay to expend this extroverted energy with others in the Social Life Room and even the Technology Room. However, we must feed the message to the Thinking Room that we should just learn how "to be" and not think too much of a certain high emotion. Be lowkey.

Life is not all sunshine and rainbows every second of the day. It is important to remember a statement while in the Thinking Room: "Life is hard." This creates a mental callous, as it is a reminder that a certain high emotion will not carve out a pleasurable path for the future in the long term.

THE CHESS ROOM (SELF-CARE AND SELF-CONTROL)

When I have an opportunity to work on a developing craft in the Chess Room, it is important I do not let my hobbies interfere. One hobby may be surfing, for example. I may go into the appropriate Miscellaneous Room and spend time surfing, which is fine. However, if this is a comfort escape from a difficult chess game at hand, then the hobby acts as comfort more than quality leisure time.

If I want to be a better swimmer, for example, then each chess game I play should be toward getting a better workout in. If I accomplish a goal I had already accomplished several months ago, then that goal has already left its gem on my inner scepter, and I cannot find comfort in achieving that same goal again and again because it is no longer one of my current intentions. In striving for more uncomfortable goals and practicing self-control in any endeavor, I must also be cognizant that I need better quality self-care.

GOOD OR BAD HAPPY?

How do we know if the joyous feelings we have at times are real happiness? If a depressed person finds comfort in the presence of another depressed person in the Social Life Room, then that is not valuable happiness. The inner scepter is not embellished because it is simply a "misery loves company" scenario.

However, if I go through the struggle of training for an exam and get an acceptable grade, this produces a valuable feeling of happiness. My inner scepter is embellished! It is important to be cognizant of our joyous feelings and gauge them to our inner scepter. A happy feeling is a happy feeling. We must search for its reasoning and analyze it in connection with the Thinking Room! For example, we can ask ourselves: "Did this joyous feeling stem from something in the Chess Room or any of the Time-out rooms?" It is okay to have a "good happy" feeling from one of the Time-out rooms, but can the source of the feeling be conducive to our intentions in the Chess Room?

PROACTIVITY INCLUDES TAKING THE STEP BACK

To be proactive means to be cognizant of the comfortable temptations that may destroy our momentum at any given point of our chess matches. The best tactic to have in the Chess Room is identical to one that any chess player has in a chess match itself: having a plan. Smart people with uncontrollable emotions will be less successful than mediocre-minded people with a plan and robust sense of self-control.

The best visualization to give in any chess match is to imagine yourself with a shield, expecting an array of rocks to be thrown at you. You have to be in a defensive state of mind and expect the worst to happen in order to prevent a burnout and gravitation toward comfort.

It is easy to envision the ideal result of any chess match. However, it is important to not indulge in this train of thought. To achieve a goal, yes, you must picture it. However, there must be a boundary set against it to a reasonable degree. The process is more important because it is what will get you from point A to point B. A good mental trick to possess in this scenario is to lift your index finger to your lips and say "shhh." This provides a subtle but strong energy to connect with the Thinking Room in a stable manner whilst in the Chess Room. Otherwise, if the end result overtakes your mentality, there is a risk of having giddy and irrational energy. Subconsciously, the mind knows what it wants based on the journey of practicing self-control in the Brain Hut!

* * *

More work requires more sleep, healthier eating, and regular exercise to keep the body functioning. It is important not to beat yourself up if you fall due to a lack of self-control. Instead, you have to get right back up and keep persisting in the Chess and Self-Care Rooms. Every move in the chess game counts. If I overcome a pleasurable temptation in the Technology Room and showed up to fight in the Chess Room, then that is a pawn move in and of itself. I must reflect on my progress in the Chess Room and question my failures: "Did I lose to Time because I succumbed to comfort, or because I failed through an organized effort?" I will know the answer by understanding my whereabouts before entering the Chess Room.

CHAPTER 4

FEAR AND IMAGINATION

———

I may remain complacent in a Time-out room and let fear prevent me from taking the first step to the Chess Room. Imagination, however, can help me combine my past ideas and experiences from any room into a new idea for Chess Room execution.

In Part Two, I stressed the importance of acknowledging the root of our fears when it comes to doing certain tasks. Perhaps they are from past emotion or they are innate, such as a fear of certain reptiles. The Thinking Room is the best weapon to harness in order to work through our fears and use our imagination.

I also mentioned the value of synchronicity in Part Two. The circumstances and scenarios around us can signify a specific meaning to each of us. But am I willing to connect with the Thinking Room in any room to digest and evaluate its reasoning and message? This is a special intention in and of itself because it can lead to a proactive calling.

THE TECHNOLOGY ROOM

In moments of boredom, the easiest escape is to navigate through the smartphone apps. However, what if we can connect boredom and the Thinking Room to exercise our imagination? Virtual devices will only suck us into a different dimension to be a consumer rather than a producer of ideas. Author Srinivas Rao says, "…in order to be able to create, we must make an effort to limit 'inflow' or the influx and consumption of data and information…through a combination of decision fatigue and decreased attention spans, constant information 'inhibits creativity, negatively impacts our ability to do deep work and reduces our cumulative output.'"[129]

Since intentions are internal, I am not going to find a magical effect from a virtual source. I can see the pretty side of success and valuable riches on a screen, but just because I obtain such images in my head does not mean I am destined to obtain them. I need to create my own rewards and think of a plan of how to get there. The self-made aspect of my imagination is what makes it feel so liberating from my fears. I just need to trust the process. If I am in the Technology Room when I should be in another room, then it is logical to simply remind myself that social media is not a good idea in the moment.

However, if I am in the Technology Room out of boredom to superfluously spend my time, then I need to learn how to embrace boredom. That is the solution. When I feel like there is nothing to do in any room in the Brain Hut, I can

---

129 "The Beauty of Boredom: How Technology Can Ruin Your Creativity," TechnologyAwareness, accessed October 9, 2020.

overcome the mundane vibe and connect with the Thinking Room. This is when the imagination aspect can do its magic for a new plan—just by being in the moment. I can't control my thoughts; instead, I must accept them and, hence, a potential transformation.

I identify one fear in the Technology Room as the fear of "sloth." When I see someone else post about a great accomplishment or a picture with smiling faces, it makes me feel like I should be "doing something" constructive. Great accomplishments or experiences take effort. I should not be in any rush to provide myself any feeling of expedient joy to rebound from the "do something constructive" feeling.

A picture of smiles indicates that the social media users are going through happy experiences. However, this is not always the case. I know people who are going through sad times who can manage to pull a smile on the screen to prove to the world they feel otherwise. Think of a half-bitten apple and a mirror, symbolizing social media. Typically, the mirror will show the unbitten side of the apple—the pretty side. The bitten and ugly side is not transparent on the mirror.

I need to use the Thinking Room and ask myself: "What is this social media user truly like in real life?" It would be an act of folly to think in many directions about what other people are doing with their lives, most of which are not arbitrarily true. To lessen fear and anxiety, I need to keep my life goals as private as possible and avoid the online competition.

Texting can be very ambiguous. Certain emojis and charismatic texts may delude the recipient into thinking the sender is communicating with passion; instead, the texts may come from a nonchalant presence. It is best to never assume how meaningful text messages are, regardless of their vibe from behind the screen. Instead, imagination is vital in mentally processing the sender's typical body language. It is better to use your best judgment through imagination in the Social Life Room rather than interpret instant messages in the Technology Room. Assumptions of someone's intentions through the Technology Room may create confusion and even fear regarding how to approach the person again in both the Technology and Social Life Rooms.

THE SILENT ROOM

In the Silent Room, it is easy to overthink. There is nothing to react to or any external cause which will propel us to use our imagination. However, in this room there is peace. The worst weapon against peace is overthinking because it creates a dark cloud which will leave us in a mental clutter. The Silent Room gives us an opportunity to take that proactive step back for self-evaluation and prevents us from jumping into any false conclusions.

There is a trick to overcoming this clutter. Just as I use soap to clean my hands from germs, I can use an empty jar and a sheet of paper to cleanse my mind. I need to tear the sheet of paper into several pieces and write one thing I am grateful for on each slip. As I insert each slip into the jar, I notice the jar gradually becomes full with every special note I place into it. This changes my perspective since I know that even the smallest blessings can liberate me from fear of action. The best part of this is that it is in the Silent Room;

hence, I have a personal base for my joy that only I can understand.

Along the Chess Room journey, however, there are people in the Social Life Room who may misunderstand me. It requires too much energy to explain myself and it is not worth doing so. The Silent Room is where my reality makes the most sense because I do not have any external aspects to interfere. The personal conversation I have with myself in the Silent Room's mirror releases me from the fear of walking down a lonely road. My imagination bursts in flavor since I feel so liberated in isolation.

This does not mean to say that the journey to success must always be lonely. It does, however, mean that one must be ready to overcome the fear of loneliness and do what is right. The Silent Room has so much privacy that it is a safe haven to reflect on one's progress in the Chess Room. It can be so tempting to go to the Social Life Room to seek validation from others in respect to my journey. I need to let go of that insecurity, establish a relationship with my inner scepter in the Silent Room, and understand its calling.

There is nothing that can destroy iron but its own rust. In the Silent Room, we are faced with the only person to fear: ourselves. We can grasp this room's mirror to imagine our future selves and harness that into our imagination for the Chess Room. This creates excitement in our personal space and a base for our own private thinking. Nobody in the Social Life Room can transfer their verbal fears to you because you subconsciously understand how and where the roots of your goals started in the Silent Room.

Meditation is a great antidote to block fear, especially in the midst of silence. In Part Two, I noted that meditation shrinks the amygdala, the part of the brain related to fear and emotion. Not only does it get rid of fear, but it also increases creativity. Meditation teacher Elleke van Kraalingen refers to a stage of meditation, saying that "mental force is being bundled to a strong potential, which may lead to the experience of deep silence and insight, and may be used for affirmation, visualization, and creative ability."[130]

Consistent meditation can hard-code a personal idea so well that it creates a purpose for whatever I do outside of the Silent Room. The subconscious mind has its own ways of giving us information from "unknown" sources, yet there has to be a connection in regards to our knowledge. Fear is reactive and, in a way, wishing for the worst to happen. Practicing positive imagination on a daily basis will help mitigate any false feelings. Optimism will be second nature!

THE CHESS ROOM

Every time I want to embellish my inner scepter more in the Chess Room, I get hit with the fear of failure. But this fear can go two ways—the good or bad fear. The bad fear of failure relates to the negative emotions from a setback. Dr. Guy Winch says, "...what separates rejection from almost every other negative emotion we encounter in life is the magnitude of the pain it elicits...brain scans show that the very same

---

130 Elleke van Kraalingen, *Meditation and Imagination* (UK: Sixth Books, 2011), 19–20, Google Books.

brain regions get activated when we experience rejection as when we experience physical pain."[131]

In these instances of fear, I need to harness the Thinking Room and transcend beyond the emotional aspect of failure. I need to focus on the "why" behind the failure. Was I moving my chess pieces too quickly before thinking? Was I single-tasking during the chess game?

A good solution for the bad fear is to understand the good fear through a specific meditation. After every Chess Room failure, I can gather my thoughts and emotions into the Silence Room. I can imagine each failure as a building block toward my meditated end goal. This changes the perspective of fear from bad to good. Either I can let this block weigh me down for good or I can use it as a lesson to rise above in my next effort.

The more I meditate on this aspect, the more my improvised move will become second nature. The fear of failure will be removed and left in the past. If I do not meditate on a failure and continue to make the same move, then the second failure is a choice. This may build an irrational fear that I may be cursed with bad luck. Meditation will build the objective perspective back and subdue the subjective.

The Chess Room does not come with instructions. It is important to walk through the room's door with not only a proactive mindset, but a proactive look as well. The more

131   Guy Winch, *Emotional First Aid: Practical Strategies for Treating Failure, Rejection, Guilt, and Other Everyday Psychological Injuries* (New York: Penguin Group, 2013), 8–10, Google Books.

formal or appropriate the dress code, the more resonant you will be in the chess match toward your end goal. Imagine yourself winning the match like a champion and dress like one!

The beginning of the chess match may stir fear in you since the chessboard looks intimidating, with only a vague outlook of which direction the match can go. However, as you continue to move fearlessly with every move, the intimidation is suppressed. A good source of confidence in the Chess Room is being cognizant of the past small victories on your success path. Imagine and think like you have been here before!

THE SOCIAL LIFE ROOM

The Social Life Room plays a good role for imagination but a bad role for fear. Synchronicity can be quite common. The right person may come to me at the right time and make a crucial statement, which will trigger my subconscious mind to deliver a meaningful idea at some point in the future. This is why I note that being in the present is so essential to improve creativity and its sources.

When I am in the Social Life Room, I do not want to enter the Technology Room or other Time-out rooms in the midst of others. Other people have different experiences and knowledge to share at the table. Words are so powerful. Even if it is just a simple and encouraging statement. Someone else may express his lessons from his own chess games, and I can connect with the Thinking Room during the conversation and imagine how it can apply to my own craft.

On the other hand, the type of people I surround myself with is worth noting as well. Negative and judgmental people can plant "bad seeds" in my Chess Room just by what they verbally convey to me in the Social Life Room. I need to have a proactive mindset to be ready to flush away these empty comments. In other words, I must hold myself accountable for burning these bad seeds before they grow into a scary presence in the Chess Room, otherwise it will only stir fear and self-contempt, hindering me from executing my goals to the best of my abilities. I cannot play the blame game and make excuses that others are putting me down. Instead, I have to master the fear of criticism and not care what other people think. Nobody else knows the full story of my personal Brain Hut agenda. They are in different rooms and doing different things from what I am doing in the Chess and Time-out rooms.

Just like I can convert the fear of failure into proactivity, I can also convert the bad seeds into stepping stones to prove to myself that I am worth adding another gem on my inner scepter. However, it requires persistent imagination and rationality. I am not going to have more conversations with anyone else than the ones I have in my head. Therefore, I need to be kind to myself and make the choice to let go of irrational fear. If you believe it, you can achieve it!

KEEP THE PEACE
We do not want to stir disruption with anyone in the Social Life Room. Therefore, it is best to find some mental tricks to sustain rapport:

- If someone has a controversial statement to share with you, be a troll. Reply with subtle sarcasm, pretending that you can compromise with his or her standpoint. However, keep the dialogue very vague.
- Pretend that you did something bad for the other person. For example, pretend you are conversing with the person after you accidently knocked down his or her cup of coffee. The whole idea is that you should feel like you are in debt of respect to the other person when you feel that tensions are running high and there is potential for fear and hostility between you.

When you want to give advice or explain something that is genuine to someone, make sure you build the process over time. It is not feasible to digest somebody else's years worth of knowledge overnight. Learning takes time and the best trait to have is a pleasant personality. Regardless of the other person's thoughts, you must be respectful and listen when good character is present. This will release any fear of judgment and false self-consciousness.

DO NOT BE FOOLED AND OBTAIN FALSE INSECURITIES
Sometimes when I see how professional a friend is in a meeting room or how fluent the friend is in speaking another language, I can feel intimidated, like I should be in the Chess Room working very hard on a new skill. This is not necessarily true. Everyone is different and has gone through a process to develop a new skill. Any superb display of knowledge is simply an emission of this training process. The person, at the end of the day, is normal and did not "grow an extra limb" to perform such actions.

Be fearless and confident that you can achieve anything you set your mind to. Everyone finds their niche at different ages in life. Fears are just thoughts we create. Do not let the Social Life Room brainwash you!

THE THINKING ROOM

In any of the rooms, the Thinking Room is important to connect with in order to exercise imagination over our fears. We want to be hypothetical in every situation and understand how it may affect our Chess Room goals. This helps us prepare for our fears in unprecedented times. For example, say I have a paper due next week. I must be proactive in knowing the weather for the upcoming week. What if the power runs out? I will need to knock down the majority of the assignment before such an event may occur whilst in the Chess Room.

We may have to react to a fight-flight-freeze situation or decide to be proactive before such a fearful occasion. Let's look into both of these concepts.

REACTIVITY WHEN IT IS TOO LATE

We may lose our control and be overtaken by such fear at times. When we feel tense in a fearful scenario, it is best to not overthink. We must remember that everything is normal. It is best to reflect in the Thinking Room about a past fearful moment in the one of the rooms. Here we are alive and breathing. If we got through a past experience, then we can get past this current one.

Usually, we want to strive to be our best selves and focus on what works for our inner scepter. Emulation can be a temporary trick to use. We can imagine what someone else in our Social Life Room may do in our current situation, somebody who is competent to take on any personal fears. We can learn from another's example, but we should never let go of our personal identity.

The Thinking Room mentality is one of risk. Either we are living—acting on our Chess Room goals—or dying—remaining complacent in the Time-out rooms—during our lifetime. The goal of life is to *live* and leave this planet with a notable mark. We must imagine our inner scepter as a beautiful masterpiece, resilient throughout all the fear produced in any of the rooms in the Brain Hut. Life will be unfair, but there is no need to be fearful of such obstacles. A good quote I meditate on is, "This is the ultimate game the Chess Room has for us: to overcome life's irrational fears to obtain our king victory."

Irony can play a role amid fear. Typically, we want the "I can do it" mentality, yet we can still prevent ourselves from taking that first step. Ironically, I can nonchalantly say, "Nope, not going to happen." In the spur of the moment, this sarcastic attitude may portray our fears as folly. In this moment, I can make that chess move spontaneously.

BE PROACTIVE

The Thinking Room is a reliable source for constructive thinking. Therefore, the more we harness it, the more potential we have to explore our imagination and bring it to fruition in a rational manner. If we want to be elite Chess Room winners, then we must think *elite*, the special power of the Thinking Room.

At the same time, we do not want to view the Thinking Room as the magical source to executing our goals. Sometimes, the Thinking Room naturally connects with us based on memory. For example, if I am learning a new swimming technique, then I am utilizing the Thinking Room to focus on how to improve and adapt to the new stroke. After a while, I do not need to stress as much in the Thinking Room since my technique will become natural. Muscle memory will keep my mindset sustainable with the Thinking Room every time I am in the water.

We can thrive off the Thinking Room seamlessly when we have obtained much knowledge from past Brain Hut room experiences on a certain goal. The subconscious mind tends to naturally give us ideas on how to act, as if we are not actually thinking for ourselves. It is best to simply trust this proactive tendency.

A failure in the Chess Room should leave us in fearful despair. Think of a broken pencil. We should not be so quick as to completely leave the Chess Room in full doubt. Instead, we should connect with the Thinking Room and decide how we can sharpen both ends of the broken side of the pencil. At the end, we have three sources of writing from the two split pencil parts that are all together.

The most efficient way to conquer fear and maintain a robust, imaginative mindset is to move forward in life with loyalty and verbal prudence. Loyalty to your chess match and to your true friends in the Social Life Room will keep your mind focused on what you want despite any irrational obstacles. It is a rare trait to have because it is easy to think that we can easily be fooled by someone else. If we practice loyalty, we are then building our character and attracting the right energy in the Social Life Room.

We want to be careful about who we share our Chess Room ideas with to prevent any bad seeds in our Brain Hut! The best proactive mindset to have is to not speak too much of our plans to anyone until we have reached the checkmate point in our chess game. It takes true loyalty and trust from someone else to share such ideas from our Thinking Room. Use the Thinking Room with profound prudence!

SYNCHRONICITY

The Thinking Room should be used to grasp the moments of synchronicity in all the rooms in the Brain Hut. Synchronicity is so subtle that it can easily be overlooked if we are not constantly thinking. In fact, if we do not fully acknowledge a special coincidence, then it can easily be laughed away as a weird occurrence rather than serving a deep message.

It was synchronicity which led to this point of writing a book.

Last year, I was lost and wanted to find the right signs to lead me to a practical passion. My drive to find a purpose in life took a different turn in September 2019 in the Technology Room. A friend sent me a text with a quote: "In the quiet places of life you will find comfort. But if you handle the quiet place poorly, then everything will go wrong." I loved the quote and asked him where it come from.

"You wrote it," he texted back.

He was quoting from an article I had written the year before. Suddenly, I realized what I wanted to do—write. The coincidence of hearing from this friend out of the blue just as I was thinking about my future was too much for me to ignore. However, I knew if I were going to be a writer, I would have to become a reader as well.

One of the first books I started reading was *Outwitting the Devil* by Napoleon Hill. One day, on the train back from work, a gentleman approached me.

"Where did you get that book?" he asked.

"Barnes & Noble," I replied. "I liked the cover."

"I've read a lot of Napoleon Hill's work," he said.

The gentleman went on to describe another one of Hill's books and recommended I read it. I asked him what his occupation was, and he stated he was a senior vice president (SVP) at a well-known company. We talked for a few minutes more and exchanged contact information. A few days later, we started a conversation online. The last thing he asked was, "If you know why God had us connect, let me know."

Although I wanted to start writing, I put it off for a week until I had finished reading *Outwitting the Devil*. The first thing I do every morning is read a daily motivational reading from a book named *Our Daily Bread*. On the morning that I sat down to begin writing, the first words in the motivational text were, "as a young writer…." The reading was about an eager, inexperienced, and young writer who was learning new skills in a classroom filled with professional writers. The story made a reference to the tale of David and Goliath, explaining how David, despite his small size, was able to defeat the much larger Goliath. The writer in this story had reminded me of my lack of writing skills the same way that the illiterate Rocky had reminded Goggins of his own illiteracy. I then thought about the man I'd met on the train. It was because of him that I'd postponed starting writing, and therefore started on the day with that particular inspirational reading. This is why God had the both of us connect. This coincidence gave me courage to go all the way with writing.

The text from my friend in the Technology Room, Mr. SVP's conversation with me in the Social Life Room, my interest in reading in the Chess Room, my ability to organize these cues in the Silent Room–all of these aspects led to *The Brain Hut*. They would not be possible without my connection to the Thinking Room. I defined imagination as the combination of old ideas into a new idea. These signs to get into writing, as well as my passion for self-help, were due to my self-awareness of the scenarios which took place around me in the Brain Hut rooms. Think and believe. The universe will have its ways of communicating back for golden opportunities to embellish your inner scepter, to give you a new passion in entering the Chess Room, a passion so big that fear cannot get in the way!

Choose One Emerald over One Hundred Stones

I am sick of pretending to validate myself to unapprecia-
tive stones.

They make me mask my insecurities, giving me chills to
my bones.

Why do I take for granted my few emeralds?

They show me support and stick with me, even in times
when the stones make me imperiled.

Life is too short to feel degraded by the stones' criticism.

I will harness my emotions to improve my humility while
they continue with egotism.

Stones act spontaneously and want to cascade bad emotions, how arbitrary!

At least my emeralds will help thicken my skin and push
me forward, on the contrary.

Skip the stones back in the pond and dig deep to find the
emeralds in your life.

For the best, long-lasting emerald you can find is your
own wife.

Be persistent and conquer the mold the stones throw in
your swimming lane,

For the stones one day will be filled with remorse while you fly above them like a plane.

You should hold onto your emerald like it is a kite.

The emerald is under your control and there is no problem in sight.

Once you decide to let go of the kite in chase of a single stone,

The emerald is completely out of control and you feel empty, all alone.

Treasure the emeralds who support you every single day.

They know you well in each and every, single way.

The stones will spread negative seeds in your Chess Room.

After, you must eliminate these contagious feelings, and sweep them out with a broom!

–Nicholas D'Souza

CHAPTER 5

STORIES

———

There are ways you can use the Brain Hut to bring self-awareness in regards to how proactive and intentional you are within a certain time frame. I will discuss the variations as I go along each of the following examples and stories. They include the principles discussed throughout the chapter.

MEL ROBBINS (MOTIVATIONAL SPEAKER)

Mel Robbins' Brain Hut story focuses on a five-second window. Robbins states that one night, she saw a rocket launching on TV and thought of an idea: she would count 5-4-3-2-1 and launch herself out of bed the next morning to overcome her habit of hitting the snooze button. The Technology Room, in this respect, exemplified synchronicity. This trick already set up a quick and easy chess game for her; she had to just make that one chess move to get Time in checkmate. There were bad seeds in the Chess Room, or her bedroom. Using her *imagination*, she was able to overcome the *fear* in her mind to be proactive every morning.

The 5-4-3-2-1 trick created a fight-or-flight reaction in her brain, a sense of urgency to react in an intense moment. After the first successful chess win, she tried it again and again every day until it became a *habit*. The trick got the mind in the right zone. It was a form of *single-tasking* since there was a single focus in that short five-second window—to get out of bed. Sleep is a form of *self-care* but staying in bed was a form of procrastination and showed a lack of *self-control*.

NICK BOLHUIS – VICE PRESIDENT OF PERFORMANCE PROGRAMS AT NEUROPEAK PRO

The Brain Hut can be a good tool to sketch one's perspective of how to approach each room. Nick Bolhuis is the vice president of Performance Programs at Neuropeak Pro. One of their goals is to evaluate brain functionality and design customized plans to help clients better manage stress. I got to interview Nick and ask him questions regarding the scope of stress in the Brain Hut rooms.

He notes that there is an innate stress we may regularly have without any reason at all. It is inevitable that our environment can be stressful. However, it is possible to overcome this type of stress. In regards to the Technology Room, Nick says that it can be stressful to hear everyone's opinions. Unless one enters the room prudently, it is best to stay out of the Technology Room.

Nick notes to be intentional in the Social Life Room and look for both people who will lift us up, and people who will bring us down. We need that balance. We need to get everything and learn from anything.

In regards to the Chess Room, Nick says that the work to get there stirs fear. In order to get there, we need to take small steps, not a big leap. He stressed the importance of neuroplasticity, the ability of the brain to form new connections and pathways and to change how its circuits are wired. I need to avoid the passive state of mind and reflect on the potential upgrade I can provide to my mindset. Nick says that in order to train the brain to beat stress, we should work through the stress rather than around it. There is no finished product, meaning that we will never attain a perpetual state of being stress free. There is an exercise in overcoming stress. Stress is natural and normal, and we should not be defined by our stress levels.

In regards to the Thinking Room, Nick states that it provides mindfulness, which involves accepting feelings and formulating an approach on how to overcome them. For example, he refers to fear. If I am scared, then I map out a plan. What can I do in the rooms to get better and feel more in the present moment? I cannot be a hamster on the wheel every time. I must thrive off honesty and work through my flaws.

JACQUES

I have a friend named Jacques. He grew up playing video games and continues playing video games even in his mid-twenties. He sets a good example for someone who prioritizes his time in the Technology Room for a quality time-out. He spent most of his childhood indoors rather than outdoors, so video games became a fun escape for him, and playing them turned into a *habit*. To this day, he lives under the same roof. He says that if he were to move out, he would probably not take his video games with him. Video games would be a distraction amid a fresh start to a new environment. The interesting point is that this perspective would not apply as much to his home because it would help him resonate with his environment as it always did when he was growing up.

On the other side of the coin, he mentions that too much time in the Technology Room may provide an excessive rush of dopamine, becoming a detriment to what is important in life. Jacques says that the best way to balance time in the Technology Room is to ask yourself the honest questions, such as: "Will this be a waste of time from doing something that is more important?" He says that as long as he does not make the video game objectives such a big deal, he will have a balanced mind when transitioning from the games to important tasks.

A key note he mentions about playing video games online with mutuals is that it is not the same as communication in the Social Life Room. He realizes that he can play with one friend for months, but they only bond over a video game rather than personal conversations about what is going on in their respective lives. This is something to be cognizant of, as there should be a separate form of communication from video games to keep a genuine bond with friends. Again, it all boils down to superficial bonding in the Technology Room.

On the bright side, Jacques says that we can learn something from the Technology Room if we keep our ears open. He notes a video game scene (from *Star Wars Knights of the Old Republic 2*) from his childhood where he gave an A.I. homeless character some money. Another A.I. character denounced such an act and told Jacques' character: "Why would you give him that money? He should take a step back and learn why he got here." Jacques realized how powerful this message was because it reflects on self-accountability. To this day, he never forgot this lesson. He harnessed the Thinking Room in the Technology Room and applies this message to his regular chess games.

FRANK

I have a former college swimming teammate named Frank. He took his second year off from swimming and made a return in his third year. He was a fast swimmer and wanted to improve a lot more to realize his true capabilities. Frank and I would do our personal lifting every Saturday outside of our regular nine practices per week. We lifted in a gym setting near the balcony of the pool.

Frank would look out the window in-between rest sessions and use his *imagination* to combine his mental and physical efforts into the final product: personal best times, medals, and school records. Each round of weights symbolized one chess move against Time. Once we got into the *habit* of lifting, it seemed that *fear* was never in the picture. As we connected the Chess Room to the Thinking Room, nothing else seemed to interfere with our respective imaginations.

A big contribution to this was our personal Silent Room and Thinking Room moments when we would reflect on our progress. Frank would think of the Social Life Room and imagine his competition whilst lifting. He did not specifically know who his competitors were, but he knew for sure he was putting in more work than they were for Championships day. Every extra lifting session, all season long, added more substance to a big gem on his inner scepter.

Frank went on to win several medals, including gold, and several school records. He credits those lifting sessions as giving him the edge for his performance. The Thinking Room was a vital component in connecting with the Chess and Silent Rooms as his thoughts came into full fruition. Frank's Brain Hut shows the power of imagination from the Timeout rooms, specifically the Social Life Room and Silent Room.

PHIL

I have a friend named Phil. Phil's Brain Hut story deals with the negative aspect of the Technology Room. After college, Phil would have a group chat with his peers to keep in touch. After two years, they decided to meet up and he felt unsettled because he had viewed them as text bubbles since college. He wished he could have used the Thinking Room more whilst in the Technology Room to articulate who they genuinely were in real life. Phil thinks the Thinking Room can be distorted—not necessarily dishonest, but a text can be interpreted in different ways. The best approach is to harness *imagination* by connecting the Thinking Room with the Technology Room to reflect on Social Life Room memories and thrive off facts.

WELDON

I had a friend named Weldon tell me about one night when he was procrastinating for a term paper that was due at midnight. Instead of harnessing the Thinking Room with the Chess Room, he was in the Technology Room watching entertaining YouTube videos. He set his *time management* to finish his paper in the Chess Room but gravitated toward the Technology Room, which was the opposite of *single-tasking* and an example of a lack of *self-control.* Every second that passed, Weldon would say, "It will be done."

There was no link to the Thinking Room, and no actual movement in the Chess Room. That paper required one lengthy chess game and Weldon, in a nutshell, was deluded into thinking his pieces would make the moves themselves. Weldon ended up never starting his paper and taking the loss due to his gravitation toward comfort. If Weldon were to look at his Brain Hut map in retrospect for that night, then he would see the clear issue—excessive time in the Technology Room.

ME

BEFORE FRESHMAN YEAR

The summer before my freshman year of college, I was fortunate for the opportunities ahead of me: a quality education and a walk-on spot on my college swim team. However, I felt that great feats would magically happen by just dreaming about them. My Brain Hut was not functioning according to the Thinking Room at all; it was just wishful thinking. That summer, I was in the Social Life Room a lot and I enjoyed my time based on pure emotions. I ignored the Silent Room and instead entered the Technology Room to spend hours and hours playing sports video games.

I did enter the Chess Room for swim practice, but I falsely believed that showing up was one hundred percent of the job.

I had no train of thought. I lacked proper sleep because I was too busy texting in the Technology Room. I established bad habits, had poor time management, no self-control, no imagination, and a fake sense of fearlessness, believing I could accomplish anything based on irrational and high emotions.

During the first semester of my freshman year, I made no improvement in swimming and played my chess games foolishly without any direction. I ended my first semester with a low GPA because I was in the Technology Room instead of doing homework in the Chess Room.

AFTER FRESHMAN YEAR

During the second semester of my freshman year, I decided I wanted to make a big change. I had to let go of the Social Life Room friends who made me feel mediocre. To establish a robust Brain Hut, I had to start primitive.

The following summer, I went into the Technology Room to search for videos on courses I knew I was taking the following semester. I did my own swim practices for most of the weeks with a deep purpose. This all subtly developed good habits in me and organized a strict schedule to follow. I stayed out of the Technology Room unless it required the Thinking Room. I completely let go of the Social Life Room because I knew what I wanted to accomplish in a few short months, and I wanted to embrace the Silent Room's mirror.

I persisted in the Chess Room each and every day through each and every failure. Imagination helped me harness these failures into new challenges. I learned a lot and made no expectations, as I just wanted to grow. I naturally had self-control because I was comfortable with being uncomfortable. I feared where I was going with it, but it was a good fear of curiosity and adventure.

Toward the end of the summer, I realized how much stronger and faster I was in the water and it paid off the next season, as I dropped three full seconds in a four-lap race. Also, after much contemplative thought for the upcoming academic semester, I was able to earn a much higher GPA, bringing up my cumulative GPA to a reasonable number.

The lessons I learned were to stay out of the Technology and Social Life Rooms unless they bring good value. It is okay to have downtime with friends, but it should be very occasional when in the middle of an intense Chess Room journey. The Silent Room should be the best Time-out room since it is a safe place to meditate and rewire the brain with the Thinking Room.

CHAPTER 6

THE THREE H'S

THE NONCOGNITIVE SKILLS

Habits, time management, self-control, self-care, fear, and imagination are all exercises we must harness for proactivity and intentionality. In a way, they all measure against Time. It is also important to note the noncognitive skills which do not acknowledge Time—the three H's: Humility, Heart, and Humor.

Life is short, and our goals in the Chess Room may make us anxious since we do not know if we will live to see the day when the real execution begins; for example, Championships day, when the culmination of our hard work in the Chess room sets us up for the grand stage in the Chess room itself. But along the way, it is important to go deeper into one's self; meaning that we are learning more about our strengths, weaknesses, and capabilities. Our character and reputation should receive acknowledgement and be treated with the same fairness as the embellishment of our inner scepter. Through our intentions, we want to inspire others. That should ultimately be the end goal of an intentional lifestyle.

This does not only pertain to a bigger community after we accomplish a new ruby for your inner scepter in the Chess Room. Within the Time-out rooms, we want to share bits and pieces with others for inspiration. In this way, we make the journey seem more realistic to others. This must be accomplished through harmony and love for the most efficient impact.

No matter how embellished your inner scepter is, there is no guarantee you will maintain a happy lifestyle. You can reach the pinnacle of a sports or business journey but still fall short from the "high" if you do not have life's meaning in the right perspective. Although I am providing the guidelines for setting goals throughout the book, I have included the "three H's" to explain the healthy balance we can have between the Time-out rooms and the Chess Room.

Ideally, Time wishes for more than an iridescent and well-embellished inner scepter. Rather, Time wishes for: *A purposeful effort to exercise the mind and body, but more importantly the heart and soul; the latter which knows no Time, no pressure, no fear, but only Love.* I will start with the caveats to the three H's, which are the seven deadly sins: lust, gluttony, greed, wrath, envy, pride, and sloth.

THE SEVEN DEADLY SINS

The Social Life and Technology Rooms should be avoided in the midst of **lust**. Just as they are with the other sins, they are vulnerable to our primitive senses. If I need to be in either room for an important circumstance, then I need to connect with the Thinking Room to overcome these innate emotions. Lust relates to other people. The Technology Room can give a more expedient temptation than the Social Life Room because of its virtual aspect.

If one connects the Thinking Room with the Social Life Room, however, the Social Life Room can actually be an escape from the temptations of lust. This also pertains to our time in the Silent Room. Loneliness can lead me into a desperate sense of insecurity, and lust could easily be an avenue to submit to "comfort." However, in the long term, this will only exacerbate my integrity and self-control. We live in a society where instant gratification seems more compelling than love throughout the heart. Our efforts in the Chess Room are ones which should be sustainable. Likewise, our love for someone else should have deep meaning and, in a way, bring value and support to our personal goals as well.

The same idea applies to *gluttony* as well. The Silent Room is a dangerous place to be in without reason. Boredom may lead to finding comfort in food. Like bad eating habits, gluttony can be hindered by surrounding oneself with friends who eat healthily. Gluttony is similar to excessive time on social media. Every time I open the fridge, I am opening my social media account. I may be doing it out of boredom and see the same news feed or food. Another time, I may be surprised by a new post or food product, but the out and in motions are not under control. They are unnecessary and provide comfort in a falsely productive aspect.

Sometimes I can get carried away with the rewards of the Chess Room. Perhaps money is a good motivator. It is unhealthy to get too sucked in to the pleasures of such rewards because they obtain no limit; such is **greed**. Everything materialistic in this world is temporary. Once we die, all our possessions are left for someone else. When entering the Chess Room, it is important to focus on the "good" greed, which is embellishing our inner scepter with as many chess victories as possible. This will produce inspiration and hunger for even more inspiration.

Wrath relates to the anger one feels when there has been a moment of injustice or even failure. Anger can feel so irrational that it is best to stay out of any of the rooms, except for the Silent Room. Wrath in the Technology Room can lead to a controversial social media post, which can receive negative commentary and a deep feeling of regret. Wrath in the Social Life Room can be detrimental to a relationship with someone else when one's dark side is revealed. The act may be forgiven, but the memory will never die. It is like a broken vase—you can fix it, but it won't look exactly the same as the original.

It also takes Time to put back the pieces and the Thinking Room to know which pieces go together. When I go to the Silent Room and see my reflection in the mirror, I want to see a composed individual who practices self-control with pleasure as well as anger. It is important to note that you should not make promises when you are happy, and you should not make decisions when you are angry. Measure twice, cut once.

Envy refers to jealousy of others' success. When someone hears about someone else's Chess Room accomplishments in either the Social Life or Technology Rooms, envy may start to arise. It is best to go to the Silent Room and reflect on how one can change himself and stay in his own lane. Everyone is different. The grass may seem greener on the other side, but one may not realize he is exactly where he should be. Great announcements are not arbitrarily announced. There was some deep work put into it, and a lot of contemplative thought in the Silent Room. Nobody else can control someone else's inner scepter, only his own. You live your world in your head. When the Social Life Room wants to put envious ideas in your head, you have to use your imagination to dodge these bullets. Envy will produce insanity, so it is best to just keep it realistic and focus on what you can control. Losers focus on other people; winners focus on progress in the Chess Room.

Pride can be both good and bad. Self-confidence is a sense of good pride. It indicates that someone knows he is worth achieving that ultimate gem in the Chess Room and will not let the bad seeds wear him down. However, there is a contradictory pride which can be present within oneself before and after a chess game. There is a false sense of pride that someone can win a chess game "just because" he feels he is worth it. Only repetition and hard work will cover the delusional holes in this false pride. The post chess game pride is relevant, especially after a significant win. The champion may move back and forth from the Technology Room to the Social Life Room, bragging about his inner scepter. This is detrimental since Time is wasted from harnessing the Thinking Room for a new series of chess games to play. It may lead to the point when the champion views his accomplishments as a great superficial past as opposed to a rigorous and genuine process.

The highs of embellishing your inner scepter may feel very powerful, but eventually they will die down. It is easy to compare your accomplishments to anyone else's in the Social Life Room. However, what happens when someone else achieves something greater than what you have over time? You will feel an urgency to seek validation by striving for better in the Chess Room. This, however, is only a way to prove others wrong. Our goals should pertain to only what we feel our abilities are worth going for.

Sloth seems to be the easy route to waste Time away from the Chess Room and do nothing. There are days when one has to take a well-deserved break after burnout. Perhaps, they need to feel rejuvenated because they lost focus, and hence, they need some contemplative thought. This example does not refer to sloth, but a reasonable excuse to be in a Time-out room.

When the mind lacks the Thinking Room, there is no opportunity for memories, and without memories, there is no opportunity for imagination. Even if it means just entering the Chess Room reluctantly, there is a possibility for a train of thought. Champions are built on the days they do not feel like entering the Chess Room. If you can show up on your weakest days, then you can build tolerance against negative feelings. Do what is right, not what is easy.

THE THREE H'S

Humility, humor, and heart are the swords to fight against the seven deadly sins. They create a deeper meaning to act upon one's goals in the Chess Room. However, a big passion will not necessarily embellish the inner scepter alone. The six principles must be exercised as well since they are closely associated with the brain. The point of the three H's is that

I cannot find it elsewhere; instead, I must be it. I can learn much from other successful people and use critical thinking for how they achieved what they have. However, it is important to not emulate their personalities. Instead, I need to observe the subtle hints of their inner wisdom. Everyone has a different purpose in their proactive lifestyle. I need to find my own within, and it all starts through my intentions.

HUMILITY

Humility keeps me based and realistic of my limitations as a human being. I must not act with pride, but I must also not act like I am completely worthless or without any significant accomplishments. The beauty of the Chess Room are the failures. They scare me because they may lead to humiliation. However, humiliation and humility are closely connected. They awaken my flaws and steer me away from the false sense of pride. Humility gives a realistic approach as to what my Brain Hut activity looks like, rather than pretending it is something I want but do not actually practice.

Essentially, the opposite of humility is pride. To gain more pride, one has to chase more chess games. However, humility will bring a composed mind into the Chess Room and have the mind work as if nothing has been accomplished before. Instead of reflecting on what you do not have, it is important to reflect on what you do have: gratitude. This will cleanse the mind and harness an approach to give rather than receive, which is the main idea of proactivity and intentionality.

It is important to never underestimate others in the Social Life Room and their value. Every connection counts. You will never know if someone has a connection to an opportunity you crave in the Chess Room. Humility will hold your chess victories at arm's length when conversing with someone. You do not want to start tension with someone based on credentials or success status. Life is short and we never know when our last day will be. We do not want to leave a bad impression on anyone before it is too late to reconcile.

Success simply amplifies what is within you. At the end of the day, you are nothing more than a human being. It is fine to celebrate the chess victories in the Time-out rooms, but do not get carried away as if you have nothing else to prove. You have to go with the mentality that there is someone out there who is better than you.

LOSER TRICK MENTALITY

I bring the "loser mentality" into the Social Life Room to mitigate any negative commentary from others. I do not view myself as a loser, per se, but I may give that impression to others due to my lack of selfish pride. When people know you are climbing the ladder, there is space below you which some are willing to bring you down to. It is best to move up the ladder and out of the view of others. Make others think you are losing but keep your good progress exclusively to the Silent Room. Do not speak until you are properly ready to exclaim, "Checkmate!"

HUMOR

Humor is a vital component to keep one's spirits alive throughout the intentions process. When we are so focused on a chess game that it is all we can think of, it is important to block out any unnecessary "noise" in the Technology and Social Life Rooms. Humor helps mitigate the seriousness of any drama and flushes it out. However, it is best if one recollects any distracting moments in the Silent Room and creates a comical narrative of it. If one was to make a public, comical statement on a certain situation in either of the other Timeout rooms, then it may be blown out of proportion by others.

With this in mind, it is important to be neither too giddy nor too dark in humor. In the Social Life Room, we are going to expect trolls and goofballs who may sidetrack us from our goals. To reciprocate, there must be a connection to the Thinking Room with a mix of elegant sarcasm. In the Silent Room, one must use humor to suppress any intense and serious thoughts of oneself. We are not meant to be looked upon as a complete joke, but we also not meant to look entitled over others. In a way, humor can assist humility as it mitigates pride. I have a belief that without humor, there is no proactivity. It is simple to fake sadness with a smile, but I would find it hard to fake it through the eyes. Humor makes the eyes smile. It creates joy and joy creates proactivity.

HEART

Heart is the main base for all intentionality, regardless if one realizes it or not. It defines purpose and meaning. When the heart is reignited, there is a strong will to do whatever it takes to get the job done, regardless of how lost someone is in the process. Where there is a will, there is a way. The "why" dominates the "how." Intentions, through the heart, innately harness the Thinking Room in whichever room the ambitious person journeys. This question stays in the mind: "In what way can this current circumstance add to my imagination later on?" The heart does not have the characteristics of the brain. It does not resonate with irrational emotions, fear, or Time. Therefore, it has resilience against the worst odds or fears.

Since the ultimate goal of our intentions is to leave a mark on the world for others, our inner scepter's degree of beauty should symbolize how we want to share our hearts to the world. Ironically, it is not our flaws, which may intimidate us on our road to influence others, but actually our deep potential to shine our light to others.

Previously, I mentioned that we should have no expectations of our goals in the Chess Room. Expectations may feel intimidating because we think of doing something which does not exist yet. Therefore, we need to live in the moment and harness internal trust and love with our hearts to overcome all irrational fear.

In trying to influence the world, we are sharing our heart with others. We want to inspire others by our beautiful scepter. By doing this, we have a special love for the other person.

What does it mean when you say you love someone? It can mean different things to different people. For me, I define love as caring for somebody else's physical well-being and soul in the afterlife. But ultimately, we should have love for everyone. It should be an honor to inspire someone else in the Social Life Room and awaken their scepter potential. Our goals should not be exclusive to our own happiness, but for others' as well.

INTENTIONALITY AND PROACTIVITY

The three H's provide more meaning and purpose to our intentions. Unjust actions against us may diminish them, but it is up to us to harness the six principles and regain the three H's along the process. Nobody will remember us by our credentials, but they will by the impact we make on them. This book stresses the six principles because they are the roots for action. The three H's may bring great emotions, well-being, and potential, but they are no use if not put into action; the six principles put the three H's into action.

The principles can be harnessed well for a temporary time, but they will eventually die if not provided with internal passion. This is why, in addition to our cognitive capabilities for our life's intentions, this conclusion provides an important mantra: *"A purposeful effort to exercise the mind and body, but more importantly the heart and soul; the latter which knows no Time, no pressure, no fear, but only Love."* No matter how successful you are in the Chess Room, the biggest question in life is: "How much love have you poured out into the Silent and Social Life Room?"

ACKNOWLEDGMENTS

———

I had quite the year-long journey writing *The Brain Hut*. There are special acknowledgments I would like to mention.

To my good friend John Landry: You set a series of synchronicity that led up to this opportunity to write this book. Thank you for everything!

To my Fordham friend JJ Meador: Thank you for connecting me with Eric's book program. This opportunity would not be possible without you!

To my best friend Joseph Mercurio: Thank you for being such an inspiration and teaching me how to live every single day with prime focus and grit.

To Georgetown Professor Eric Koester, New Degree Press Head of Publishing Brian Bies, my Developmental Editor Katie Sigler, my MRE Kristy Carter, and my fellow NDP authors: Thank you all for your encouragement and guidance in this process. This would not be possible without all of you!

A special shout-out to my Beta Reader community who supported my presale this past summer, including my family, friends, swim teammates, colleagues, fellow brothers from Seton Hall Prep, and fellow Rams from Fordham University!

Adam Arafat

Aidan Anthony Rodricks

Alan Lopez

Aldrin Pinto

Alex Tunaru

Alexa Cucchiara

Allan DGuerra

Anna Daccache

Andres Polanco Achury

Andrew Glockenmeier

Anesia James

Anjana Sreedhar

Ann Alemao

Anthony Figueroa

Ashley Boren

Bertrand Anty

Brandon Paul

Brandon Posivak

Brandon Wang

Brandon Weir

Brenda Ziegler

Brendan Barrett

Brian Utkewicz

Carter Frazee

Catherine Chen

Christopher Indudhara

Colleen D'Souza

Craig Nazareth

Daniel DeMeo

Debra Weigand

Deirdre Nazareth

DenMark Clarke

Derek Daly

Dermot Bree II

Dmitriy Zakharov

Drew Baldauf

Drew Dembek

Dylan McMurrer

Eileen McCarthy

Elizabeth Jeong

Emily Shipley

Emmanuel Laoye

Enoch Kurimella

Eric Koester

Erik Tseng

Esther Kim

Faeez Juneja

Frank Bozzi

Giselle Gomes

Gloriana Restaino

Grace Singrick

Grant Durner

Herving Grullon

Ishah Tariq

Jack H. Burke

Jack Brennan

James McElduff

James Hooper

James Milone

James Savage

Jared Furtado

Jarrod Schwesinger

Jeremy Joachim

Jesse J. McMullan

Jessica McCubbin

JJ Meador

Joan Singrick

Joao D'Souza

John Landry

Jon Hanlon

Joseph Bellantuono

Joseph J. Mercurio

Joshua Graziani

Julia Alemao

Julia Paul

Justin Dunn

Kailey Walters

Kalena Laurent

Kate Bernauer

Kurtis Rossie

Kyle Kroen

Latasha George

Lee D Klein

Lichuan Wang

Lisa Ginder

Madeline Parlato

Malcolm D'Souza

Mariela Tejeda

Marissa Rodrigues

Matthew Masino

Melroy J. Lopez

Melvyn Lopez

Michael Alemao

Michael Bertelle

Michael Condon

Michael G. Gallo

Michael Muha

Michael Rasile

Michael Savignano

Miguel Mattox

Mikaila Ullal

Nathaniel Arlequin-Aleem

Neal Patel

Nicholas Lugo

Nick Alemann

Nick Belfanti

Nicole Ruckert

Nicole Spindler

Patricia Logan

Patrick Keyes

Paul Ingrassia

Peter Abrahamsen

Peter Oppizzi

Phil Bedard

Phillip Jones

Phillip Wilcox

Pranav Satyal

Priyanka Surio

Rajan Nicholson Vaz

Raphaella Clump

Rebekah Alemao

Rev. David Pickens

Rhett Karopoulos

Richard Baum

Rinette Morris

Russ Lopez

Ryan Hackett

Ryan Mellody

S. Mayumi "Umi" Grigsby

Samantha Foulston

Samir Ullal

Sammy Rogers

Samuel Wayland

Sarah Skelton

Scott Paul Brown

Sean Anukwuem

Sean Finlay

Shintaro Noguchi

Shirley Wayland

Shobha Dasari

Simona Edward

Sonia Perez Arellano

Sorab Panday	Tamar Haddad	Tommy Ajayi
Stephanie Crowley	Tavish Boyle	Valarie Discafani
Stephanie Roddy	Ted Sales	Valerian Sequeira
Stephen Lewandowski	Thomas Dabish	Valerie Oliva
	Thomas E. Slattery	Vincent Chan
Sudhir Ullal	Tiffany Mosher	Vincent Natoli
Sunny Khanna	Tom Nascone	Vinita Ullal
Sydney Welch	Tom Nascone	Zenon Niewada

APPENDIX

INTRODUCTION

JRE Clips. "Joe Rogan —David Goggins Journey From 300 lbs to a Navy Seal." February 19, 2018. Video, 22:25. https://youtu.be/HVi3oPufVPg.

PowerfulJRE. "Joe Rogan Experience #1080 —David Goggins." February 19, 2018. Video, 1:54:22. https://youtu.be/5tSTk1083VY.

PART 1 CHAPTER 1

Barker, Eric. *Barking Up the Wrong Tree: The Surprising Science Behind Why Everything You Know About Success Is (Mostly) Wrong.* Harper One, 2017. Google Books.

Dweck, Carol S. *Mindset: The New Psychology of Success.* New York: Penguin Random House, 2006, 2016. Google Books.

PART 1 CHAPTER 2

Drummond, Norman. *Step Back: Why You Need to Stop What You're Doing to Really Start Living.* UK: Hodder & Stoughton, 2015. Google Books.

Eurich, Tasha. *Insight: The Surprising Truth About How Others See Us, How We See Ourselves, and Why the Answers Matter More Than We Think.* New York: Penguin Random House, 2017. Google Books.

Locke, John. *An Essay Concerning Human Understanding.* Indianapolis: Hackett Publishing Company, 1996. Google Books.

Markman, Art. *Smart Change: Five Tools to Create New and Sustainable Habits in Yourself and Others.* New York: Penguin Group, 2014. Google Books.

Peterson, Jordan. *12 Rules for Life: An Antidote to Chaos.* Toronto: Penguin Random House Canada Limited, 2018. Google Books.

Steel, Piers. *The Procrastination Equation: How to Stop Putting Things Off and Start Getting Stuff Done.* HarperCollins e-books, 2010. Google Books.

PART 2 CHAPTER 1

Astor, Tamsin. *Force of Habit: Unleash Your Power by Developing Great Habits.* Florida: Mango Publishing Company, 2018. Google Books.

Covey, Stephen R. *The 7 Habits of Highly Effective People.* Miami: FranklinCovey, 2015. Google Books.

Dean, Jeremy. *Making Habits, Breaking Habits: Why We Do Things, Why We Don't, and How to Make Any Change Stick.* Massachusetts: Da Capo Press, 2013. Google Books.

Duhigg, Charles. *The Power of Habit: Why We Do What We Do in Life and Business.* New York: Penguin House, 2012. Google Books.

Fuchs, Oswald. *The Psychology of Habit According to William Ockham.* Oregon: Wipf and Stock Publishers, 2016. Google Books.

O'Connor, Richard. *Rewire: Change Your Brain to Break Bad Habits, Overcome Addictions, Conquer Self-Destructive Behavior.* New York: Penguin Group, 2014. Google Books.

Prochaska, James O., Carlo C. DiClemente, and John C. Norcross. *Changing for Good: A Revolutionary Six-Stage Program for Overcoming Bad Habits and Moving Your Life Positively Forward.* Harper Collins, 2010. Google Books.

Schwartz, Jeffrey M. and Rebecca Gladding. *You Are Not Your Brain: The 4-Step Solution for Changing Bad Habits, Ending Unhealthy Thinking, and Taking Control of Your Life.* New York: Penguin Group, 2011. Google Books.

PART 2 CHAPTER 2

Dawson, Peg and Richard Guare. *The Smart But Scattered Guide to Success: How to Use Your Brain's Executive Skills to Keep Up, Stay Calm, and Get Organized at Work and at Home.* New York: The Guilford Press, 2016. Google Books.

Kabat-Zinn, Jon. *Full Catastrophe Living: Using the Wisdom of Your Body and Mind to Face Stress, Pain, and Illness.* New York: Bantam Books, 2013. Google Books.

Sterner, Thomas M. *The Practicing Mind: Bringing Discipline and Focus into Your Life.* California: New World Library, 2012. Google Books.

Newport, Cal. *Deep Work: Rules for Focused Success in a Distracted World.* New York: Hachette Book Group, 2016. Google Books.

Panda, Satchin. *The Circadian Code: Lose Weight, Supercharge Your Energy, and Transform Your Health from Morning to Midnight.* New York: Penguin Random House, 2018. Google Books.

Rosen, Larry D., and Adam Gazzaley. *The Distracted Mind: Ancient Brains in a High-Tech World.* Massachusetts: The MIT Press, 2016. Google Books.

Saunders, Elizabeth Grace. *The 3 Secrets to Effective Time Investment: Achieve More Success with Less Stress.* China: McGraw Hill Companies, 2013. Google Books.

Seppala, Emma. *The Happiness Track: How to Apply the Science of Happiness to Accelerate Your Success.* San Francisco: HarperOne, 2016. Google Books.

Tracy, Brian. *Master Your Time, Master Your Life: The Breakthrough System to Get More Results, Faster, in Every Area of Your Life.* New York: Penguin Random House, 2016. Google Books.

USCDornsife. "To Multitask or Not to Multitask." Accessed September 5, 2020. https://appliedpsychologydegree.usc.edu/blog/to-multitask-or-not-to-multitask/.

Vyshedskiy, Andrey. *On the Origin of the Human Mind*. MobileReference, 2014. Google Books.

Zack, Devora. *Singletasking: Get More Done—One Thing at a Time*. California: Berrett-Koehler Publishers, 2015. Google Books.

PART 2 CHAPTER 3

Gelperin, Roman. *Addiction, Procrastination, and Laziness: A Proactive Guide to the Psychology of Motivation*. Roman Gelperin, 2017. Google Books.

Lustig, Robert. "The Hacking of the American Mind with Dr. Robert Lustig." Filmed September 2017 at University of California. Video. 32:42. https://robertlustig.com/hacking/.

McGonigal, Kelly. *The Willpower Instinct: How Self-Control Works, Why It Matters, and What You Can Do to Get More of It*. New York: Penguin Group, 2012. Google Books.

Mischel, Walter. *The Marshmallow Test: Mastering Self-Control*. Little Brown Spark, 2014. Google Books.

Newport, Cal. *Deep Work: Rules for Focused Success in a Distracted World*. New York: Hachette Book Group, 2016. Google Books.

Oberparleiter, Lee. *The Role of Emotion and Reflection of Student Achievement*. Indiana: AuthorHouse, 2011. Google Books.

Peterson, Jordan. *12 Rules for Life: An Antidote to Chaos*. Toronto: Random House Canada, 2018. Google Books.

PART 2 CHAPTER 4

Carbonell, David A. *The Worry Trick: How Your Brain Tricks You into Expecting the Worst and What You Can Do About It*. California: New Harbinger Publications, 2016. Google Books.

Chopra, Deepak. *The Seven Spiritual Laws of Success: A Practical Guide to the Fulfillment of Your Dreams*. California: Amber-Allen Publishing, 1994. Google Books.

Dingman, Marc. *Your Brain, Explained: What Neuroscience Reveals about Your Brain and its Quirks*. UK: Nicholas Brealey Publishing, 2019. Google Books.

Dutta, Dr. Sanchari Sinha. "Hippocampus Functions." News Medical. Accessed September 7, 2020. https://www.news-medical.net/health/Hippocampus-Functions.aspx.

Fletcher, Emily. *Stress Less, Accomplish More: Meditation for Extraordinary Performance*. HarperCollinsPublishers, 2019. Google Books.

Hanh, Thich Nhat. *Fear: Essential Wisdom for Getting Through the Storm*. Harper One Publishers, 2012. Google Books.

Pittman, Catherine M., and Elizabeth M. Karle. *Rewire Your Anxious Brain: How to Use the Neuroscience of Fear to End Anxiety, Panic, and Worry*. California: New Harbinger Publications, 2015. Google Books.

Puff, Dr. Robert. *Reflections on Meditation: A Guide for Beginners.* California: Ebookit.com, 2011. Google Books.

Schaub, Friedemann. *The Fear and Anxiety Solution: Guided Practices for Healing and Empowerment with Your Subconscious Mind.* Colorado: Sounds True, 2012. Google Books.

Shumsky, Susan. *Awaken Your Third Eye: How Accessing Your Sixth Sense Can Help You Find Knowledge, Illumination, and Intuition.* New Jersey: The Career Press, 2015. Google Books.

Simpkins, Annellen M., and C. Alexander Simpkins. *Meditation and Yoga in Psychotherapy: Techniques for Clinical Practice.* New Jersey: John Wiley & Sons, 2011. Google Books.

Subba, Desh. *Philosophy of Fearism: Life is Conducted, Directed and Controlled by the Fear.* Desh Subba, 2014. Google Books.

Vilhauer, Jennice. *Think Forward to Thrive: How to Use the Mind's Power of Anticipation to Transcend Your Past and Transform Your Life.* California: New World Library, 2014. Google Books.

PART 2 CHAPTER 5

Amen, Daniel G. *Change Your Brain, Change Your Body: Use Your Brain to Get and Keep the Body You Have Always Wanted.* New York: Harmony, 2010. Google Books.

Arden, John B. *Rewire Your Brain: Think Your Way to a Better Life.* New Jersey: John Wiley & Sons, 2010.

Dingman, Marc. *Your Brain, Explained: What Neuroscience Reveals about Your Brain and its Quirks*. Massachusetts: Nicholas Breasley Publishing, 2019. Google Books.

Huffington, Arianna. *The Sleep Revolution: Transforming Your Life, One Night at a Time*. New York: Harmony, 2016). Google Books.

Masley, Steven, and Jonny Bowden. *Smart Fat: Eat More Fat. Lose More Weight. Get Healthy Now*. Harper Collins, 2016. Google Books.

McGonigal, Kelly. *The Joy of Movement: How Exercise Helps Us Find Happiness, Hope, Connection, and Courage*. New York: Penguin, 2019. Google Books.

Mosconi, Lisa. *Brain Food: The Surprising Science of Eating for Cognitive Power*. New York: Penguin Random House, 2018. Google Books.

Ramsey, Drew, and Tyler Graham. *The Happiness Diet: A Nutritional Prescription for a Sharp Brain, Balanced Mood, and Lean, Energized Body*. Rodale Books, 2012. Google Books.

Walker, Matthew. *Why We Sleep: Unlocking the Power of Sleep and Dreams*. Simon and Schuster, 2017. Google Books.

PART 2 CHAPTER 6

Galindo, Javy W. *The Power of Thinking Differently: An Imaginative Guide to Creativity, Change, and the Discovery of New Ideas*. California: Enlightened Hyene Press, 2009. Google Books.

Gilbert, Elizabeth. *Big Magic: Creative Living Beyond Fear*. New York: Penguin Random House, 2015. Google Books.

Jung, Carl. *Jung on Active Imagination*. New Jersey: Princeton University Press, 1997. Google Books.

Pressfield, Steven. *The War of Art: Break Through the Blocks and Win Your Inner Creative Battles*. New York: Rugged Land, 2002.

Surprise, Kirby. *Synchronicity: The Art of Coincidence, Choice, and Unlocking Your Mind*. New Jersey: The Career Press, 2012. Google Books.

PART 3 CHAPTER 1

Markman, Art. *Smart Thinking: Three Essential Keys to Solve Problems, Innovate, and Get Things Done*. New York: Penguin Group, 2012. Google Books.

PART 3 CHAPTER 2

Covey, Stephen R. *The 7 Habits of Highly Effective People*. Miami: FranklinCovey Co., 2015. Google Books.

Hill, Napoleon. *Think and Grow Rich*. think-and-grow-rich-ebook. com, 2007. http://roblewis.com/wp-content/uploads/Think-And-Grow-Rich_2008-10.pdf

Kuss, Daria J., and Mark D. Griffiths. *Internet Addiction in Psychotherapy*. England: Palgrave Macmillan, 2015. Google Books.

Newport, Cal. *Deep Work: Rules for Focused Success in a Distracted World.* New York: Hachette Book Group, 2016. Google Books.

Rosen, Larry D., and Adam Gazzaley. *The Distracted Mind: Ancient Brains in a High-Tech World.* Massachusetts: The MIT Press, 2016. Google Books.

Turkle, Sherry. *Reclaiming Conversation: The Power of Talk in a Digital Age.* Penguin Books, 2015. Google Books.

PART 3 CHAPTER 3

Latona, Valerie. "The Big Benefits of Exercise Buddies." AARP. Accessed October 9, 2020. https://www.aarp.org/health/healthy-living/info-2019/exercising-with-a-partner.html.

Newport, Cal. *Deep Work: Rules for Focused Success in a Distracted World.* New York: Hachette Book Group, 2016. Google Books.

PNAS. "Evening use of light-emitting eReaders negatively affects sleep, circadian timing, and next-morning alertness." Accessed October 9, 2020. https://www.pnas.org/content/pnas/112/4/1232.full.pdf.

Sheldon, Pavica, Philipp A. Rauschnabel, and James M. Honeycutt. *The Dark Side of Social Media: Psychological, Managerial, and Societal Perspectives.* UK: Elsevier, 2019. Google Books.

Simon, Julie M. *When Food is Comfort: Nurture Yourself Mindfully, Rewire Your Brain, and End Emotional Eating.* California: New World Library, 2018. Google Books.

PART 3 CHAPTER 4

van Kraalingen, Elleke. *Meditation and Imagination.* UK: Sixth Books, 2011. Google Books.

TechnologyAwareness. "The Beauty of Boredom: How Technology Can Ruin Your Creativity." Accessed October 9, 2020. https://technologyawareness.org/2016/11/08/the-beauty-of-boredom-how-technology-can-ruin-your-creativity/.

Winch, Guy. *Emotional First Aid: Practical Strategies for Treating Failure, Rejection, Guilt, and Other Everyday Psychological Injuries.* New York: Penguin Group, 2013. Google Books.